D0776872

To _____

_____

_____

From _____

Date _____

God's Whispers
to a
Woman's Heart

Cindi McMenamin

HARVEST HOUSE PUBLISHERS
EUGENE, OREGON

Cover by Dugan Design Group, Bloomington, Minnesota

Cover photo © Yuri Arcurs—Fotolia

GOD'S WHISPERS TO A WOMAN'S HEART
Copyright © 2014 by Cindi McMenamin
Published by Harvest House Publishers
Eugene, Oregon 97402
www.harvesthousepublishers.com

ISBN 978-0-7369-5450-1 (padded HC)
ISBN 978-0-7369-5451-8 (eBook)

Printed in China

17 18 19 20 21 / RDS-JH / 10 9 8 7 6 5

For Sarah—
Thank you for giving me the privilege of
watching your faith grow as you recognize
Him working in your life and listen for
His whispers on your heart.

Preparing to Hear His Voice

Do you long to hear God's whispers on your heart? To know His thoughts of you, His plans for you, His comfort and His presence? Chances are He is already whispering. You and I just need to get quiet enough to listen. That's what this book will, prayerfully, help you do. I have divided it into three sections to help you recognize His whispers, reflect on His character, and respond to His heart.

Part I: Recognizing His Whispers—God communicates through the Scriptures. By reading them and picturing His heart for you, you will prayerfully learn to recognize His voice through His Word.

Part II: Reflecting on His Character—Sometimes it may seem like God isn't there. But He often makes His presence known to us by what we experience on a daily basis. This section will help you look for His presence and listen for His whispers in your everyday circumstances.

Part III: Responding to His Heart—As you reflect on God's Word and His character, your response will no doubt be one of worship, wonder, and ultimate surrender.

So quiet yourself and listen closely, dear friend, to what God is whispering to *your* heart.

Listening for Him alongside you,
Cindi McMenamin

PS: Hearing God's whispers on your heart begins when you have a personal relationship with Him. To find out more about what that means, see "Surrendering Your Heart" on page 169.

Part I

Recognizing His Whispers

*Open your heart and listen to Him
whisper through His Word...*

Listen for My Whispers

*Whether you turn to the right or to the
left, your ears will hear a voice behind
you, saying, "This is the way; walk in it."*

ISAIAH 30:21

Are you hoping for guidance today? Do you want to know how to walk in My ways? Then quiet down, My child, and listen for Me. I am the One who is beside you every moment of the day, providing direction, whispering affirmation, nudging you to show love toward others, pulling you back from harm. You need only to quiet yourself and listen for My loving voice. I will not intrude upon you, nor frighten you, nor discourage you. My voice is not in a terrifying wind, nor in a startling earthquake, nor in a consuming fire. Listen for Me in the sound of a gentle blowing, a still small voice (1 Kings 19:11-12).

Lord, I long to hear Your whispers that warn me, direct me, and affirm me of Your comforting presence. Train me to hear Your voice, not the distracting one that leads me astray.

Look for Me…and Find Me

*You will seek Me and find Me when you
search for Me with all your heart.*

JEREMIAH 29:13 NASB

I'm aware of the days when you're hoping to hear something from Me. My child, I whisper thoughts and encouragement on your heart all day long. I am the One who longs for *you* to listen. You hear so many distracting thoughts and words that can drown out My voice: your doubts, your own negative thoughts, the critical words of others, taunts from the enemy. Start looking for Me in your daily circumstances. Listen for My whispers in the kind words of others. Feel the peaceful assurance of My presence as you go through your day. You *will* find Me—and hear from Me—when you search for Me with all your heart.

*Lord, tune my ears to hear You alone, not my own
doubts or fears or the criticism of others. I long to see
You at work in my circumstances and to hear Your
gentle whispers on my heart.*

I Understand

For you created my inmost being;
you knit me together in my mother's womb.

PSALM 139:13

Have you ever considered that it's no accident that you feel the way you do right now? I fashioned you in your mother's womb, and I knew the circumstances that would play out in your life to cause you to feel alone or anxious today. Not only have I ordained all your days and written them out before one of them came to be (Psalm 139:16), but I have a plan—and a purpose—in what you may see as your pain or plight. Whatever comes your way today has not taken Me by surprise. I have let life lead you to a place of longing or frustration so you will be reminded that I am all you need.

Will you trust Me with all that is on your mind—and in your way—today?

Lord, thank You for knowing all about what this day holds. Remind me, when I start to get frustrated or feel like I am alone, that You are right here with Me.

I Have a Plan

You saw me before I was born. Every day of my
life was recorded in your book. Every moment
was laid out before a single day had passed.

PSALM 139:16 NLT

I know you sometimes feel like your life is not going according to plan. But your life is right on track, My child. You just need to remember *whose* plan it is!

I see all your expectations, but I hold the ultimate blueprint in *My* hands. I looked down through the ages of time and knew what you would need to become more intimately connected with Me. And then I ordained your days—overseeing your circumstances, and providing enough of Myself to be available to you when you feel you're at your wits' end, so you will see Me as your All in All. Will you trust Me with everything that is happening in your life right now?

Lord, You hold my life in Your capable hands. I trust
that You know what You are doing, and You will
engineer my circumstances in whatever way will keep
me closest to You.

You Are Precious

How precious are your thoughts about me, O God.
They cannot be numbered!
I can't even count them;
they outnumber the grains of sand!
And when I wake up,
you are still with me!

Psalm 139:17-18 nlt

Did you know, My child, that I am constantly thinking of you? The number of thoughts I have for you cannot even be measured. And not only do I have your life story planned out, but because I love you immeasurably, that story is truly a good one.

Will you go through this day differently knowing that I am the Writer of your story and I have precious thoughts of you too numerable to measure? And will you trust Me today that I have this chapter of your life already resolved and am waiting for you to see the benefits of trusting Me as you live through it?

Thank You, Lord, that the circumstances of my life are no accident. Because You are the Writer of my story, You can get me safely to my "happily ever after."

I Will Fight for You

*The LORD will fight for you; you
need only to be still.*

EXODUS 14:14

I am ever aware of the times you feel defeated, worried, stressed out about something you can't control. I have already walked through all of the days that were ordained for you and I can keep your heart calm, your soul at peace, and your circumstances under My control. You need only to be still.

When you are anxious and trying to work through so many details, you rob yourself of experiencing My peace. I am the One who holds back the water from the heavens and parted the Red Sea. I have brought fire down from heaven and yet saved men in the midst of a flaming furnace. Surely I will not let the rivers sweep over you or the fire set you ablaze (Isaiah 43:2). Trust Me, My child, to fight for you. Be still…and watch Me come through (Psalm 46:10).

Lord, You are far more capable than I give You credit for. Teach my heart to be still as I wait for You to show Yourself strong on my behalf.

That Inconsolable Longing

You have searched me, LORD, and you know me…
you are familiar with all my ways.

PSALM 139:1,3

I know you experience that inconsolable longing. Every day of your life there is that aloneness, an incompleteness, a longing to feel deeply and truly known. You wonder at times if you have *anyone* with whom you can commune in love.

When you focus on that inconsolable longing, it will bring you down. No one on this earth—not a parent, husband, child, or close friend—will be able to know you completely. But you are known to *Me*.

Nothing else and no one else will satisfy. So bring to Me those longings that remain unmet. I am waiting to fill *your* inconsolable heart with My peace and unworldly joy. I long for you to be able to say as the psalmist did: "Whom have I in heaven but you? And earth has nothing I desire besides you" (Psalm 73:25).

Lord, thank You that my inconsolable longing is truly consolable in You. May my unmet longings on this earth increase my yearning for heaven.

Your Heart's Desire

Delight yourself in the LORD;
and He will give you the desires of your heart.

PSALM 37:4 NASB

I see what your heart longs for today. But, My precious child, why would I give you the one thing that would keep you from coming back to Me? I know what I'm doing—even when it seems like I'm withholding. I have a plan. I want you to be independent of this world and dependent on Me. I will allow the struggles that will keep you clinging to Me because I know when you are holding tightly to Me you are experiencing true joy and peace. Make Me your heart's delight, and I will put *My* desires in your heart and delight in granting them.

Hold me close, Lord, and when I start to want something more than I want You, keep me in check and draw my heart back to Yours. Increase my desire for You alone. I know that, in return, You will give me joy.

Your Search for Love

For your Maker is your husband,
the LORD of hosts is His name.

ISAIAH 54:5 NKJV

I know those deep longings within you to love and be loved completely.

I see the longings of the single woman waiting for the love of her life. I see the longings of the married woman, wondering when her husband will connect with her and make her feel complete. And I see where *you* are today in *your* longings as well.

Cry out to Me to fill the longings of your heart. My answer is always the same: I am here. Waiting to be the One to satisfy you, complete you, fulfill you. Waiting for you to learn what I have been trying all these years to show you.

The alone times in your life are meant to drive you to Me—the Only One who can satisfy. Will you start looking to Me to be your Spiritual Husband?

Lord, You are the One for me. On days when I seek something—or someone—more than You, remind me that I already have all that I am longing for.

New Beginnings

Anyone who belongs to Christ is a new person.
The past is forgotten, and everything is new.

2 CORINTHIANS 5:17 CEV

I know when you want to start over, and it thrills My heart. I specialize in fresh starts and new beginnings. I made a world that starts anew every day with sunrise. Every week has a first day to it. There's a first of every month and a New Year's Day to celebrate the birth of every year. I knew you would need fresh starts... as often as every 24 hours! In fact, I knew you'd need them even more often than that so I provided you with ample opportunities for new beginnings. With each new day you have a reminder that you can try again, get another chance, make a clean start.

Be assured that you are new not only the day you receive My love and follow Me, but you are continually new as you remain in Me.

Lord, thank You for new beginnings...the one You made in my life as well as the numerous ones You make possible as I follow You daily.

A Clean Slate

Create in me a clean heart, O God,
And renew a steadfast spirit within me.

PSALM 51:10 NKJV

Bring your heart before Me, My child. I see your broken heart from poor choices, wrong thoughts, careless words. I know you desire to wipe the slate clean. Know that I have already made you as clean as you will ever be.

I don't just clean you when you initially come to Me and surrender your life to Me (2 Corinthians 5:17). I give you a fresh start every day—every time that you see the need to start over. Every time you want to make it right with Me again.

Because you are human, you will still mess up at times. Even though you love Me and set out to do what's right, you will still fall short of My standard of perfection. That's why a new start awaits you anytime you ask.

God, thank You for the clean slate that exists when
I trust in Your Son and His righteousness that He
attained for me when He died for me on the cross.

A Fresh Start

God, make a fresh start in me,
shape a Genesis week from the chaos of my life...
Bring me back from gray exile, put
a fresh wind in my sails!

PSALM 51:10-12 MSG

My servant, David, prayed that prayer after lusting after a woman, committing adultery with her, and murdering her husband—one of his best soldiers—to cover up his sin. Yet in his brokenness, he wanted a fresh start. And I gave it to him.

No matter what you have done, when you ask Me for a fresh start, I will give it to you too. And I will make everything new. Everything. Your mind—to think pure thoughts. Your body—to live purely once again. Your mouth—to speak words that heal. Your heart—to seek after a straight path.

Do you, too, want a fresh start? Then tell me about it. I'm ready to put a fresh wind in your sails.

Lord, You know every offense I've ever committed, and all my future offenses as well. Yet your loving-kindness and mercy found a way to create in me a clean heart and a fresh start. For that, I love You.

No More Regrets

As far as the east is from the west,
so far has He removed our transgressions from us.

PSALM 103:12 NKJV

It breaks My heart to see you carry around regrets. When you confess your sin, you can live free of regret— forever. That's right. I hurled your sins further than the California coast is to the Jersey shore. From centuries past into a million years hence. As far as sunrise is from sunset. Go ahead. Try to find them. You can't. They're irretrievable. And that's the point.

With regrets in your rearview mirror, My child, there's no place to go but straight ahead—onto a new road, toward a new direction, into a new day, with a fresh new start. Follow Me. I'll lead you there.

Lord, I need to let go of the regrets that I hold deep in my heart. May they teach me what to do better next time, but no longer haunt me with a dread of my past. Create a new me right before Your eyes. And throw that old me (and those regrets) right back to where they can never be retrieved.

No One Else Satisfies

Satisfy us in the morning with your unfailing love,
that we may sing for joy and be glad all our days.

PSALM 90:14

Do you wake in the morning already satisfied because of who I am and what I have done in Your life?

There is no one on this earth who completely understands you like I do. There is no one who can love you purely and perfectly as I can. I am the Only One who is incapable of disappointing you. You need look no further: I am the Only One who satisfies.

As long as you are hoping for lasting fulfillment through intimacy with a person on this earth, you will be disappointed. All are mere men. All have sinned. And all will let you down at one time or another. When you desire Me more than anything or anyone, you will soon find that you *already* have all that you desire.

Lord, place in me a deeper desire for You so that I can truly say, "Earth has nothing I desire besides you" (Psalm 73:25).

I Strengthen Your Heart

My flesh and my heart may fail, but God is
the strength of my heart and my portion forever.

PSALM 73:26

My child, I know when you feel halfheartedly about something. Even fainthearted. At times, brokenhearted. You cannot keep your heart from being broken. It is part of the residue of living in this sin-cursed world. And there are days you cannot infuse energy into your tired soul. But I breathe life into the lifeless and energy into the listless. Although you may feel like giving up because of boredom, disappointment, or a fear of failure, I am the One who can strengthen you for the task, and help you stay the course. Whether you need strength today to keep loving someone who has hurt you, to keep working for someone who doesn't appreciate you, or to keep pursuing a goal that looks overwhelming, look to the Only One who has gone before you into that very situation. Trust *Me* to get you through.

Lord, strengthen my heart and remind me today that
You are my portion forever, and therefore I have hope
for whatever lies ahead.

Share in My Peace

Peace I leave with you, my peace I give you.

John 14:27

My child, so much exists in a single day to rob you of peace. An insurmountable to-do list. A stack of bills. A flurry of "What ifs?" Yet My Son left you with the kind of peace that can get you through *anything*.

As He was getting ready to leave this world, His disciples were apprehensive. They didn't want to face life without Him. They had so many questions, concerns, and *fears*. Persecution lay ahead of them. All but one would be martyred for their faith. They needed encouragement, strength, and hope. Most of all, they needed peace.

Watch how My Son did it. He was at peace with all things, even though He was facing the cross. He knew His Father was in control, so He was able to offer peace to those around Him. I am controlling all that *you* face today too.

Jesus, grant me Your peace that knows no fear or anxiety. Help me to live like You did...fully confident that Your Father has everything under control.

Peace as Jesus Gives

I do not give to you as the world gives.
Do not let your hearts be troubled
and do not be afraid.

JOHN 14:27

I am so unlike the world when it comes to My gift of peace. The world gives with condition. The world gives circumstantially. The world gives and then takes away. But when I give peace, it's different—without condition, regardless of circumstance, and so much better than anything you've ever experienced in this world. So you have nothing to fear.

I bless those who are mine "with peace that no one can completely understand. And this peace will control the way you think and feel" (Philippians 4:7 CEV).

You need peace today, My daughter, that controls the way you think and feel—peace that you can't understand, but that will disable anxious thoughts and make you realize you are enclosed in My comfort and care.

God, grant me Your peace to control the way I think
and feel. Govern my life with it so others will know
that I belong to You.

My Comfort for You

He heals the brokenhearted
and binds up their wounds.

PSALM 147:3

Are you experiencing heartache you believe will never subside? Are you looking at fresh, open wounds you believe will never heal? I am asking you to trust in My peace and My comfort, which can touch your life in a way that nothing else can.

There are times I will hug you through the warm embrace of others. There are times I will send out healing from My Word to penetrate your heart. There are days you will hear a song and sense that I am singing it over you. And there are times I will send My peace to cover you and comfort you like a warm blanket when it seems nothing else can get through to you.

When you need peace that transcends all understanding, know that I am already working on your behalf. Trust Me. And receive My comfort with open arms.

Lord, I want to receive Your healing touch. Cover me
with Your peace like a warm blanket. Surround me
with Your presence and Your love.

Worry About Nothing

*Don't worry about anything; instead, pray
about everything. Tell God what you need,
and thank him for all he has done. Then
you will experience God's peace, which
exceeds anything we can understand.*

PHILIPPIANS 4:6-7 NLT

What worries you today, My child? A financial situation? Silence from a friend? A doctor's diagnosis? This world is full of fears that assault you. Yet My Word instructs you to tell Me what you need and thank Me for all I've done. Then you will experience My peace.

When you tell Me what you need, you aren't informing Me. I already know all about your needs. But by telling Me, and thanking Me for My track record, as well as for what I am going to do, you are reminding yourself that I am in control. As you pray, you will be ushered into My presence, where there is peace.

*Father, I give to You everything that concerns me today:
my worries, fears, doubts, plans, reservations, and
expectations. I long to have Your peace that surpasses
anything I can understand. And I long for the peace
that assures me that You are in control.*

Experience My "More than Enough"

I have God's more-than-enough,
more joy in one ordinary day
than they get in all their shopping
sprees. At day's end I'm ready
for sound sleep, for you, God, have
put my life back together.

Psalm 4:7-8 msg

Are you looking at others and wondering when your ship will come in? Are you focusing on what you *don't* have? I have gone to prepare a place for you. "I will come again and receive you to Myself; that where I am, *there* you may be also" (John 14:3 nasb).

I have blessed you "with every spiritual blessing in the heavenly places in Christ" (Ephesians 1:3 nasb). You are a joint heir of all there is! You have an inheritance and a future! That is *more* than enough. And that is cause for "more joy in one ordinary day than they get in all their shopping sprees."

Can you draw strength from knowing that *you* have more than enough?

Thank You, Lord, for all that I have but don't necessarily see. May I see it as Your "more than enough" for me.

Let's Rest Awhile

Jesus said, "Let's go off by ourselves
to a quiet place and rest awhile."

MARK 6:31 NLT

My Son would go off by Himself at times to escape the demands and distractions of this world. But mostly to commune with Me. He missed My voice, so He would find quiet places where We could commune together again. I long for *you* to miss My voice too.

I know you get tired. And yet every day I long for you to find a quiet place so you can hear My voice and reflect on My words. What do you need to leave for later so you can simply rest and enjoy My presence today?

Even if you are not lying down, even if there is still noise in your home or office, you can rest in the knowledge that you are Mine and let Me put a song in your heart. Just praising Me will lead you to a quiet place in your heart, where you can feel rested in Me.

Lead me, Lord, to a quiet place in my heart, where the two of us can rest.

In Lonely Places

As a result, Jesus could no longer enter a town
openly but stayed outside in lonely places.

MARK 1:45

My Son knew what it was like to stay in lonely places. At times He sought quiet and lonely places to avoid the draining demands of people, and to regain His focus in the midst of distractions. But mostly, He wanted some alone time with Me.

You tend to shun "lonely places." The thought of them makes you sad. Could you seek them out, like Jesus did, so you could spend more time with Me? When you are constantly surrounded by people, you are easily influenced by what they think of you, and concerned with the words they say that sting you, and overwhelmed at the demands that they place upon you. Learn what it means to stay in lonely places with Me.

Lord Jesus, draw me to a lonely place where I can clear
my mind, enjoy some rest, and commune with You. I
know You have been waiting to meet me there.

A Day Worth Rejoicing In

*This is the day which the LORD has
made; let us rejoice and be glad in it.*

PSALM 118:24 NASB

Did you notice, My child, that My Word doesn't say:
"This is the day the Lord accidentally let slip through
the heavens; let us tolerate it and be done with it"?
Rather, it says *this* day—even if frustrating things happen—is a day that I have made and therefore it is one
worth rejoicing in. I want you to realize that even when
uncomfortable or disappointing things happen, it is
still a day in which you live, breathe, and exist. It is still
a day I have ordained for you. It is still a day in which I
walk alongside you.

Can you find something in this day worth rejoicing
about? If not, then simply rejoice. This *is* the day that I
have made—for you to live it alongside Me. See if *that*
doesn't change your outlook—and your day.

*Thank You, Lord, for this day…regardless of what it
brings my way. You have made it, and my heart sings
that You are experiencing it alongside me.*

Calling Me Your Husband

"In that day [after their restoration],"
declares the LORD,
"you will call me 'my husband'; you will
no longer call me 'my master.'"

I allowed My people, Israel, to experience struggles. My goal was not to see them suffer, but to win them back to My heart. I wanted them to see Me not only as their Lord, but as their "husband."

I long for you, also, to know what it's like to call Me your "husband"—because of how I've ministered to you in your darkest hour. Because of how I've provided for you when you would have otherwise been at a loss. Because of how I've shown tenderness toward you more than any other person has.

Trust Me through the deserts I allow you to experience. I want you to no longer see Me as a *master* whom you *have* to serve, but as a *husband* whom you *love* to serve.

Lord, teach me what You want me to learn through
whatever struggle or frustration You are allowing in
my life. I want to come out of it lovingly referring to
You as "my husband."

Never Will I Leave You

"Never will I leave you; never will I forsake you."
HEBREWS 13:5

Whenever you may feel alone, be assured, My child, you are not. It may look to *you* like you are by yourself when you are surrounded by strangers in a crowded airport, or stranded in your car by the side of the freeway, or sitting in your living room chair in a quiet house, or stressing about a meeting or appointment you are not ready for. But the fact is you are never alone. I am always there beside you. I have made a promise to you that I will never leave you nor let you out of My sight. Even on days when it appears that everyone else has walked out on you, I never will.

Thank You, Lord, for Your ever-present staying power. Thank You, too, that there is nowhere I can go where I will be without You. Just as You have promised to never leave me, seal my commitment to never wander from You.

I Go Before You

There is a friend who sticks closer than a brother.
PROVERBS 18:24

Whatat are *you* facing today, My child, that you think you're going into alone? What are you dealing with that you thought no one else knew about or understood?

I stand ready to go into that situation not just *with* you, but *before* you…leading the way. I offer you a VIP escort…and I have taken it upon Myself to be your Personal Bodyguard.

Some are fascinated by the thought of a bodyguard or celebrity escort or even a guardian angel. But why would you ever need anyone or anything else when you have Me—the Lord God—at your side? I have already seen all that you will experience today, and I will be right beside you, protecting you, delivering you, and guiding you back home.

Lord, thank You for being the Shepherd of my heart and the Protector of my Soul. I have a Personal Bodyguard in You…and that is far better than anything the world boasts of.

I Don't Make Mistakes

He is the Rock, his works are perfect,
and all his ways are just.

DEUTERONOMY 32:4

Admit it, My child. You've second-guessed me—on more than one occasion. As if your way of working out a situation would have been far better than Mine. Even though you sometimes can't see it, My ways are perfect. I am incapable of making a mistake. I see the beginning and the end, the temporary and the eternal. So I *never* make mistakes.

Will you trust Me with what looks like inconvenient timing? Will you trust Me with your world turning upside down if that is the case? Will you trust that I am in control and I wouldn't have things any other way right now? I know what I'm doing in all that I'm allowing in your life right now. And I will complete the work I have begun in you until the day of Christ Jesus (Philippians 1:6).

Lord, help me to trust You every step of the way so I don't lean on my own understanding, but rest in the shadow of Your wings.

Let's Settle This

"Come now, let us settle the matter," says the LORD.
"Though your sins are like scarlet, they
shall be as white as snow."

ISAIAH 1:18

Are you still struggling with something I've forgiven you for long ago? Some hurtful words said to someone you love? A choice made that still haunts you? Let it go. I have.

Trust Me when I say that your offenses from the day you were born were covered by My Son's death on the cross. Nothing remains on your record if you are trusting in My Son's death for the payment of your sins.

Will you let Me take care of the offenses that still haunt you? If so, you can live with the peace that there is nothing in your past, present, or future that My Son's death on the cross could not cover completely.

Thank You, Jesus, for the sacrifice You made on my behalf...so that I can have a clean slate. Help me go through this day living like one who is forgiven.

Bring Me Your Brokenness

The sacrifices of God are a broken spirit;
a broken and a contrite heart, O
God, You will not despise.

PSALM 51:17 NASB

I see the "sacrifices" that you make when you are feeling badly. I hear the resolutions in your mind: *I will pray longer, I will try harder. I will read my Bible more.* Yet the sacrifice I desire is a broken and repentant heart—one that says, "I am lost without You."

I want you to see sin the same way I do...as a disease that had to be eradicated through the sacrifice of My Perfect Son. I want your heart to break at what breaks My heart. To obey Me is better than sacrifice (1 Samuel 15:22). So when you want to please My heart, bring me yours that is broken.

Lord, thank You that Jesus was the Ultimate Sacrifice on my behalf. Help me to remember that my repentant heart and my love and trust in Your Son is all that You ask of me.

Let Me Calm Your Heart

Search me, God, and know my heart;
test me and know my anxious thoughts.

PSALM 139:23

I see your anxiety, My child. It's in your old nature to worry—to play out the "What ifs" and create different scenarios in your mind. But it is in your new nature to trust Me. That's why I want to calm your heart and clear out your anxious thoughts.

Your anxious thoughts are the thoughts independent of Me. They are the thoughts that have you stressed out, tied up in knots, wringing your hands, worrying. When you are having anxious thoughts, you are not trusting in the One true God. You are leaning on your own reasoning or someone else's. You are trusting in yourself or someone else to come through for you. Give Me credit where it's due. I know how to take care of you.

Search me, God, and reveal to me any anxious
thoughts that aren't calmed by Your presence. Reclaim
the throne of my heart so I trust You for all I need.

My Sufficient Grace

My grace is sufficient for you, for my
power is made perfect in weakness.

2 Corinthians 12:9

I know you feel overwhelmed at times. You worry that you can't get through it alone. But you don't have to. You can do all things through Christ who gives you strength (Philippians 4:13). That means I am right here, alongside you, in whatever you need to do today—carrying you, strengthening you, empowering you. My words to My servant Paul ring true for you, too. I know each time you try to do something in your own strength you will fail. But I stand ready to do through you what is beyond you. So depend on Me and you will find that as weak or incapable as you may feel, I am at My strongest in you when you are feeling your weakest.

Lord, it is Your strength I need. Empower me to face today with the confidence that not only do You go before me, but You are also able to handle whatever comes my way and enable me to complete the task.

Trust My Timing

Humble yourselves, therefore,
under God's mighty hand,
that he may lift you up in due time.
Cast all your anxiety on him
because he cares for you.

1 PETER 5:6-7

This world will ultimately treat you as it treated Me. But see it as a chance to relate to My heart and trust in My timing to lift you up in due time. I see when you do the right thing, yet it isn't appreciated or rewarded. I'm aware of your anxiety when someone else prospers—by breaking the rules—while you and your honesty appear to be overlooked. But trust Me. I have not forgotten you. There is a timing factor to all you are going through. If you are humbling yourself and I am not exalting you, your time hasn't yet come. Wait on Me, not your circumstance. I will lift you up...*in due time.*

Lord, help me to keep doing the small things in Your presence, knowing that You see my heart and will exalt me when it's time. I trust Your timing...and I trust You.

Be Fully Content

Godliness with contentment is great gain.

1 Timothy 6:6

You experience joy when you are content with what you have. How I long for you to be content with Me alone. Are you wishing you had more money? You are rich in relationship with Me. Do you feel you have few belongings? I have promised in My Word that I will supply *all* your needs according to My riches (Philippians 4:19). You may consider your home a humble one, but you are heir to a heavenly estate. And when you feel you lack energy for the task at hand, wait upon Me, and you will gain new strength. You will rise up with wings like an eagle (Isaiah 40:31).

Lord, on those days when I start wishing I had more, gently remind me of what I already have now, and what is yet to come. Carry me, Lord, on eagles' wings to the place where I am content and joyfully singing that I have all that I need.

In Due Time

The eyes of all look to You,
and You give them their food in due time.

PSALM 145:15 NASB

My child, I know that as you look around you see so many who seem to have so much more than you. But look closely. Do they have *Me*? Let Me change your heart and perspective so that you will gladly live with a little and honor Me, rather than choose to have plenty and disregard Me. Trust that I will lift you up *in due time.* Walk closely next to Me, My child, during these days that seem unfair, so that you will see Me in all of your circumstances and grow in unwavering trust. I know you desire to please Me and delight your heart in Me. As you do, it pleases Me to pour out blessings to you…in due time.

Lord, I want to trust Your timing, Your will, and Your
ways. Keep my heart humble, and keep me in a place
where I desire You more than anything else.

Come to Me

Come to Me, all who are weary and heavy-laden,
and I will give you rest...For My yoke
is easy and My burden is light.

MATTHEW 11:28,30 NASB

Are you tired? Worn out by serving? Feeling you have so far to go in being able to fulfill all that I require of you? Then come to Me and lay it down. My yoke is easy and My load is light. All that I require of you is that you love Me with all your heart, soul, and mind, and that you love others as yourself (Matthew 22:37-39). Let go of what this world says you must do to please Me, and instead look to My Son. He pleases Me. When You love Him with all your heart and trust that what He did on the cross for you was enough, I am pleased.

Lord God, help me to live lightly and freely, knowing
that what Your Son did for me at Calvary was enough.
I want to follow You closely out of love and gratitude
for what Jesus did on my behalf.

Come Away with Me

*[Jesus] said to them, "Come with me by yourselves
to a quiet place and get some rest."*

MARK 6:31

Oh, the thought of getting some rest. I know it appeals to you. And yet every day I offer you that invitation. I'm the One who puts that desire in your heart to find a quiet place to relax. I tug at you to get away with Me alone somewhere so you can hear My whispers on your heart. Find a quiet corner of the room, sit in your car during your lunch break, or seek out a park bench where you can hear the birds and feel the breeze. You can slip away with Me in your heart—no matter where you are—to a place of peace, rest, and trust.

Come, My child. I've been waiting. And now that you're here…there is much I want to tell you.

*Thank You, Jesus, for wanting to spend time alone with
me. Don't let me forget how important it is for me to
find my quiet place and invite You there to commune
with me.*

My Hiding Place

You are my hiding place;
You preserve me from trouble;
You surround me with songs of deliverance.

PSALM 32:7 NASB

I am aware of the times you want to just hide away—away from the distractions, the demands, the stressfulness of life.

My servant David, who needed physical protection at times, sang "GOD's my island hideaway, keeps danger far from the shore, throws garlands of hosannas around my neck" (Psalm 32:7 MSG). And I can be *your* "island hideaway" as well—anytime you need to sense My presence and My peace. Anytime you need Me to surround you with songs of deliverance. Anytime you need to feel loved and cherished.

She is mine. She is loved. She is fearfully and wonderfully made. Those are the songs I surround you with. Songs of who you are to Me. So, hide away in Me. And listen for My whispers through My songs.

Lord, You truly are my island hideaway. Quiet my heart so I can hear Your songs surrounding me.

Suffering Loss

*My ears had heard of you but
now my eyes have seen you.*

Job 42:5

My servant Job suffered much, losing everything he had. Prior to his suffering, Job knew *about* Me. He knew I was the Maker of heaven and earth. He knew what his father and grandfather and great-grandfather had told him. But he had only *heard* of Me. Through his pain and suffering, Job finally "saw" Me by *experiencing* Me. He saw My majesty, My power, My glory. And he was transformed in the process.

I want you to know Me in a way that transforms you. I want you to experience Me as your Provider, Sustainer, Comforter, Joy. So trust the ways I choose to reveal Myself to you.

*Lord, I don't want to have to lose it all before I realize
You are my All in All. Help me to surrender to You
before the pain, not as a result of it. I want to seek
You during days of comfort, not just days of adversity.
And help me to realize that loss leads to a deeper
understanding of Your character, Your deliverance,
Your grace.*

Indescribable

*My ears had heard of you but
now my eyes have seen you.*

JOB 42:5

Do you want to truly *know* Me? To experience My power, My presence, My gentleness, My love? Then don't be afraid of the perspective that pain will bring into your life. Job had to experience indescribable pain before he came face-to-face with the Indescribable One. Realize that through indescribable pain, *you* can come to know the Indescribable One too.

God, I am one who has heard of You. But I truly want to see You, to experience You, to know You intimately. As I walk through life, may I look to the One whom Scripture describes as "a sun and shield" (Psalm 84:11). May I cling to the One who is called the Rock and my Refuge (Psalm 62). May I trust in the One who is called Faithful and True (Revelation 19:11). Lord, make Yourself known to me during this time in my life. And may I constantly search for new words and ways to describe the Indescribable One.

Just for a Night

Weeping may endure for a night,
But joy comes in the morning.

PSALM 30:5 NKJV

Realize, dear child, that your weeping may seem like one long night, but joy will follow just as certain as the morning.

I know you wonder why you have to experience tears at all. Because, My daughter, you are not yet home. And because sometimes, through your tears, you gain a greater understanding of who I am.

My servant Job said, "The LORD gave and the LORD has taken away. Blessed be the name of the LORD" (Job 1:21 NASB). I want you to take the bitter from Me as well as the blessing. I want you to be able to say, as Job did, "Though he slay me, yet will I hope in him" (Job 13:15).

Praise Me in the pain…and watch for the morning. It *will* come.

Teach my heart, Lord Jesus, to trust in You and hope for
You through what seems like a long, dark night. Help
me to remember Your promise that joy will *come, just*
as certain as the morning.

Be Still

Be still, and know that I am God.

PSALM 46:10

Be still, My child, and know that I am God. I spoke these words to a warring nation to let them know I was the One who would fight their battles and give them the victory. It was My mighty arm that would save them and not their own efforts. And yet I whisper these words to you today to still your heart and let you know that I am the One who fights *your* battles too. I am the One who gives you victory every time you experience success. It is My mighty arm that saves you and not your own striving.

Be still, My child, in a world that demands that you constantly strive and stress. Know that I am God in a world that is trying to convince you that you can't be sure about anything. Let me do what I do best. And you learn to simply be still.

Lord, still my heart so I truly know You are God and You will fight for me.

Sensing My Love

*This is how God showed his love among us: He
sent his one and only Son into the world that
we might live through him. This is love: not
that we loved God, but that he loved us and
sent his Son as an atoning sacrifice for our sins.*

1 JOHN 4:9-10

I know you struggle sometimes with feeling My love
and My presence. On those days when you don't *feel*
My love for you, will you look, instead, at the facts?
Will you focus on the truth that My Son went to the
grave and back to get you for His own? Only one Man
could do that for you. And one Man did—2000 years
ago. Remember that. Hold onto that. And *feel* the love.

*Thank You, Lord, for not only telling me in Your Word
that I am Your beloved, but showing me, through
Your actions. No greater love exists than the love You
demonstrated for me when You gave up Your life for
me so that I could be redeemed and live eternally with
You. You have shown me, abundantly, how much You
love me. Now help me to show You how much I love
You in return.*

The Good Things

*How abundant are the good things
that you have stored up for those who fear you,
that you bestow in the sight of all,
on those who take refuge in you.*

PSALM 31:19

Think for a moment about the good things that I have given you: your life, your breath, your loved ones who bring joy to your life, your cherished moments. Even the praise and recognition you receive from others is something that ultimately comes from Me.

As you get busy, you can so easily forget your blessings. But don't forget. And remember that some of the "good things" I have stored up for you have not yet been given. They are still stored up, awaiting the moment when I choose to lift you up in the sight of all. Humble yourself in My sight, and I will lift you up at the proper time (James 4:10).

Lord, You are most pleased by my faith...not only in You, but in Your perfect timing. I trust that You have good things stored up for me and You know exactly when they will be mine.

Everything You Need

*His divine power has given us everything we need
for a godly life through our knowledge of him
who called us by his own glory and goodness.*

2 PETER 1:3

Are you frustrated that you can't live the life of obedience and purpose to which I have called you? I have given you everything you need to be obedient and productive in every way. I have given you...

- A new nature to replace your old one
  (2 Corinthians 5:17).
- The ability to withstand—or escape—temptation (1 Corinthians 10:13).
- The power to forget what is behind you and look forward to what is ahead of you as you press on for Me (Philippians 3:13-14).
- Power through My indwelling Holy Spirit, which serves as My guarantee of your eternal inheritance in Christ (Ephesians 1:13-14).

I thank You and praise You, Lord Jesus, for giving me everything I need to live a godly life. Thank You for Your Word that instructs me, Your presence that encourages me, and Your Holy Spirit that empowers me.

Your Sun and Shield

The Lord God is a sun and shield;
the Lord gives grace and glory;
no good thing does He withhold
from those who walk uprightly.

Psalm 84:11 nasb

I want you to know Me as your Sun and Shield. The sun gives light, illuminates, provides direction, and brings warmth. Yet it is stronger and more powerful than you realize. That is what I am for you…your Light to show you the way, your Illumination to give you insight, your Direction so you don't lose your way, Your Warmth to comfort you.

I am also your Shield—the One who protects you from the battles you fight in your mind, and the One who shields you from the flaming arrows of the evil one (Ephesians 6:16). There are times when you sense only darkness and wonder where I am, but I am always present, keeping you in My care.

Lord, help me to trust You as my Sun and Shield and
the One who will not withhold from me what is truly
and eternally good.

Know My Voice

*My sheep hear My voice, and I know
them, and they follow Me.*

JOHN 10:27 NASB

How I long for you to hear Me. I long for you to recognize My voice telling you to slow down, or to wait for what I will reveal to you next. Your fears are loud and they often drown out My voice. So are the critical voices of others whom you want to please. But if you would tune your ears to My voice and know it when you hear it, you would be able to follow Me more closely.

Lord, how long I have listened to other voices over Yours. I've studied others' voices to discern their tone, intention, and unspoken words. Yet Your voice is the one I truly need to be familiar with. Tune my ear to the sound of Your voice. Make me sensitive to it in the midst of the crowd, in the flurry of activity, in the silence of despair. Help me to wait for Your voice, and to move swiftly once I hear it.

Align Your Heart with Mine

Since, then, you have been raised with Christ,
set your hearts on things above, where Christ is,
seated at the right hand of God.

COLOSSIANS 3:1

You have been raised up with Me to no longer live like you used to. You are no longer spiritually dead. You are now a redeemed woman, a joint heir with Me. So set your heart and desires and passions on what will last forever. Cultivate your relationship with Me. Grow in your unconditional love for others. Look for ways to show My love to those you are least likely to love... to those who most need to see Me. Don't worry any longer about managing your reputation or gaining the approval of others. You have the approval and pleasure of the Living God, through your connection with Christ. Live like that is enough.

Lord, set my heart and mind on things above. Don't let me waste time on idle pursuits. I want to think, speak, and live like a joint heir of heaven.

Number Your Days

Teach us to number our days,
that we may gain a heart of wisdom.

Psalm 90:12

I have numbered your days, My child, and written them out in a book long before you came into existence (Psalm 139:16). I know exactly how many days you will live on this earth and what you will do with those days. I understand the brevity of your life on earth, but I want *you* to understand it. I want you to live carefully and wisely, making each moment count. Relish each breath, cherish each day, and make sure you love and live to the fullest before each sundown.

Lord, none of us knows when our last day on this earth
will be. We all have limited time to make an impact
while we're here. So, as the psalmist prayed, help me to
number my days that I may live wisely and well. May
I consider each day as if it were my last so that I leave
a legacy that brings glory to Your name.

Worth More

*Are not two sparrows sold for a penny? Yet not
one of them will fall to the ground outside
your Father's care. And even the very hairs of
your head are all numbered. So don't be afraid;
you are worth more than many sparrows.*

MATTHEW 10:29-31

I am aware of every sparrow that falls to the ground.
Not one of them falls before its time, or outside of My
good and perfect will. And I am also aware of every
"fall" in *your* life as well. I see each disappointment, failure, frustration, setback, and crisis. *Nothing* takes Me
by surprise.

Yet you tend to worry—about your provision, your
safety, your success, your reputation. Why would I not
care for you when I care down to the very last detail for
even the birds of the air?

*Lord, thank You for seeing it all and caring more than
I can imagine. You are familiar with my comings
and goings, my thoughts, and my fears. I am secure
knowing my life is in Your trustworthy hands. Forgive
me for worrying rather than resting and rejoicing in
Your loving care.*

All Your Longings

All my longings lie open before you, Lord;
my sighing is not hidden from you.

<small>PSALM 38:9</small>

Daughter, I know everything about you. Not only have I examined your heart to know your thoughts, your anxieties, your insecurities, and your doubts, but I also know every secret longing of yours as well. Some of those longings are good—your longings to please Me, to encourage and inspire others, to be the kind of woman whom others admire. But some of the longings deep within your heart are not good. They stem from unsatisfied areas of your flesh that need My healing touch. I know what is at the root of those unhealthy desires, and I can meet you there and turn those longings into something that will be glorifying to Me, not destructive to you.

Lord, take every longing and desire within me and direct it toward You. Thank You that "You open Your hand and satisfy the desires of every living thing" (Psalm 145:16).

Your Confidence

You have been my hope, Sovereign LORD,
my confidence since my youth.

PSALM 71:5

I have been whispering words of encouragement to you most of your life, dear child. You probably never realized it was Me. On those days when you felt happy, loved, confident—even as a child—it was Me whispering words of affirmation over you. When you felt you could take on the world, that was Me pushing you forward into what you were designed to do. When you were feeling scared or timid as a child and you felt that nudge to be bold, that was Me whispering, "You can do it."

You, Lord, have been my hope and my confidence, the One protecting me and cheering me on since my childhood. Thank You for being near me throughout those days, even at times when I didn't acknowledge You or notice Your presence. It gives me great confidence today knowing You've been with me all my days.

Come Boldly

*Let us come boldly to the throne of our gracious
God. There we will receive his mercy, and we
will find grace to help us when we need it most.*

Hebrews 4:16 nlt

My child, I know there are times you shrink back, thinking that if you present something to Me *one more time* I will quit listening. Or if you ask My forgiveness for the same thing *one more time* I will be angry and withhold it. But I won't. You have My ear—and My heart. You will not hear an impatient voice…only whispers of My comforting presence and My love.

I am Your Father, and I want you to tell Me what is on your heart, even when I've heard it before. I delight in your persistence. I extend grace in light of your humility…and inability. So come. Tell. Pour it out honestly. And be heard.

Thank You, Lord, that Your Word lovingly says "we should come bravely before the throne of our merciful God. There we will be treated with undeserved kindness, and we will find help" (Hebrews 4:16 cev).

Be Assured

*Whoever has my commands and keeps
them is the one who loves me.*

JOHN 14:21

I know this world, as well as the lies of the enemy, can cause much confusion in your heart and mind about whether or not you are really Mine. But this is how I know you are Mine. "If anyone loves Me, he will keep My word; and My Father will love him, and We will come to him and make Our home with him" (John 14:23 NKJV). "Remain in my love. If you keep my commands, you will remain in my love, just as I have kept my Father's commands and remain in his love. I have told you this so that my joy may be in you and that your joy may be complete. My command is this: Love each other as I have loved you" (John 15:9-12).

Lord, may it be evident to all that I am really Your child through my obedience to You and through my expression of love toward others You have placed in my path.

Much More to Say

*I have much more to say to you, more
than you can now bear.*

JOHN 16:12

As I was preparing to go to My death on the cross, I
told My friends that there was much more I wanted to
say to them. But their minds and hearts could not hold
it all. A day was coming when they would be scattered
and afraid. But I sent My Spirit to guide them into
truth. He reminded them of everything I told them.
He comforted their hearts.

My Spirit will guide you into the truth and comfort
you as well. And just as I had more to tell them, I have
much more to say to you too. Can you quiet yourself,
go to My Word, and with a soft and opened heart hear
all that I want to say to you?

*Lord Jesus, open my ears to hear what You want to
say to me today through Your Word, through my
circumstances, and through Your whispers on my heart.*

Every Part of You

*Offer every part of yourself to him as
an instrument of righteousness.*

ROMANS 6:13

I desire that you be completely Mine. Can you offer Me:

- your passion for pleasure
- your longings for love
- your drive for success
- your desire to be noticed
- your every desperate thought?

Don't worry that I will waste or mistreat what you offer Me. I will use it for My purposes, and you will experience the kind of joy that comes from being wholly Mine. The apostle Paul referred to this as offering your bodies as a living sacrifice and he equated it to "your true and proper worship" (Romans 12:1).

"Do not conform to the pattern of this world, but be transformed by the renewing of your mind" (Romans 12:2). That's how I work through you—when I transform and renew your mind.

Lord, I want to be completely Yours for whatever You have in mind. Take all of me—my thoughts, desires, attitudes, and longings.

Give Freely

Each of you should give what you have
decided in your heart to give,
not reluctantly or under compulsion,
for God loves a cheerful giver.

2 CORINTHIANS 9:7

I want to bless you, My child, "so that in all things at all times, having all that you need, you will abound in every good work" (2 Corinthians 9:8). I want you to have a consistent lifestyle of generosity, giving freely to others of your time, talent, and treasure. As you do, I will give freely to you. I will not only give, but abundantly bless you. "You will be enriched in every way so that you can be generous on every occasion, and... your generosity will result in thanksgiving to God" (2 Corinthians 9:11).

Remember, I am the God who is able to do exceedingly abundantly above all that you ask or think, according to the power that works in you (Ephesians 3:20 NKJV). Will you take Me up on that offer?

Lord, I want to be a cheerful giver. Help me to be generous with others so I can see You pour it on in my life too in ways I never imagined.

My Grace Is Sufficient

My grace is sufficient for you, for my
power is made perfect in weakness.

2 CORINTHIANS 12:9

I know there are certain things about yourself that you don't like. They make you feel inferior, incapable, and weak. Yet those things about you afford Me the opportunity to show Myself capable and strong through you. Don't be afraid of those areas in which you lack confidence. Make Me your confidence. Don't be afraid to step out in My name. Rely on My strength. My power is most visible in a vessel that is weak. My servant Paul said, "That is why, for Christ's sake, I delight in weaknesses, in insults, in hardships, in persecutions, in difficulties. For when I am weak, then I am strong" (verse 10). You can delight in your weaknesses as well...as you listen for My whispers empowering you with strength.

Lord, what makes me think I am incapable of
anything at all when I have You as My Strength, My
Confidence, and My Enabler? Be strong in me today...
for Your glory.

Guard Your Heart

Above all else, guard your heart,
for everything you do flows from it.

Proverbs 4:23

Everything you think and eventually do flows from
your heart. It is your center. Your heart—and what it
allows in—determines the course of your life. So keep
a diligent watch over it. Carefully guard your thoughts
and feelings. What you give your heart over to can
eventually control you. And you are safe and satisfied,
in perfect hands, when I am the One controlling your
heart, your thoughts, and your affections.

Protect your heart at all costs by laying everything
before Me and letting me filter out what may and may
not enter. Think of your heart like a walled city—the
castle in which I dwell. Battles will ensue to claim your
heart. But it belongs to Me. Trust Me with all that
you encounter today. I will keep you safe as you guard
your heart.

Lord, give me the wisdom and the diligence to guard
my heart so that I let nothing in that doesn't meet Your
standard.

Let Me Handle It

Better a patient person than a warrior,
one with self-control than one who takes a city.

PROVERBS 16:32

I know there are situations in your life right now that frustrate you. I know there are people in your life who are difficult to deal with too. Trust Me with those situations and relationships. Many times I want to change your perspective and grow in you a humble and patient character. While it's easier to speak your mind than hold your tongue, I desire that you trust Me and My timing. Your self-control and character-building is more important to Me than the end result of this situation that plagues you.

Lord, You told Your people "in quietness and trust is your strength" (Isaiah 30:15). Help me to lay all that concerns me at Your feet, trusting You will show me the amazing things You can do through me in Your strength, not mine. Thank You for Your promise: "I will keep you safe if you turn back to me and calm down. I will make you strong if you quietly trust me" (Isaiah 30:15 CEV).

Your Defense

"No weapon that is formed against you will prosper;
and every tongue that accuses you in judgment you
will condemn.
This is the heritage of the servants of the LORD,
and their vindication is from
Me," declares the LORD.

ISAIAH 54:17 NASB

Know this, My child—that when someone contends with My beloved, they contend with Me. When others accuse you without reason and attempt to judge your motives, they have made an accusation against Me. And I will deal with them. Your heritage is My defense when you are wrongfully accused on behalf of your righteousness. "Any accuser who takes you to court will be dismissed as a liar. This is what GOD's servants can expect. I'll see to it that everything works out for the best" (Isaiah 54:17 MSG).

Thank You, God, that I have a Defender I can count on. When it looks like terror is at my door, help me to remember that You are the One who guards the door and whatever comes my way will have to first go through You.

Part II

Reflecting on His Character

*Listen for His whispers
in your everyday circumstances...*

The Edge of Desperation

My God will meet all your needs
according to the riches of his glory in Christ Jesus.

PHILIPPIANS 4:19

Have you had one of those weeks—*or months*—when it seems like God has gone on vacation while you've been hitting the rough times? When my husband stepped out of his pastoral job for an unpaid one-year sabbatical, after eight months I began to wonder if God had forgotten about us.

Where are You, God? We can't keep living on so little. We need *You to intervene now!*

Yet God wanted to take us to the edge of desperation—where we truly needed Him—and there He reminded us that He's been right there with us all along. God may be leading you to a place where you have to depend on Him as your Provider. He knows if we have everything we want right when we want it, then we no longer *need* Him. And we're not truly desperate for Him.

Lord, make me desperate for You...not for what You give, but simply for who You are. Give me peace that You will meet all my needs.

Singing in the Desert

I will lead her into the wilderness
and speak tenderly to her.
There I will give her back her vineyards,
and will make the Valley of [Trouble]
a door of hope. There she will respond
as in the days of her youth,
as in the day she came up out of [bondage].

HOSEA 2:14-15

God used an analogy of a lovesick husband leading his wife back to his heart when He told the prophet Hosea His strategy for getting His people to turn back to Him. I wonder if God doesn't take the same strategy with us today. Could He be allowing you to go through a desert (in your finances, or your job, or your personal life) so He can "speak tenderly" to you and show you a new side of Himself—so He can show you a door of hope in your Valley of Trouble and cause you to sing again? Then don't miss it.

Lord, help me to discover a new side of You in this desert, and may I come through it singing again.

No Fear

*There is no fear in love. But perfect
love drives out fear...*

1 JOHN 4:18

What desert is God allowing you to walk through so He can show you a new side of Himself? Could He be taking you through a desert of loneliness so you will see Him as your "spiritual husband"? Could He be allowing you a trek through the wasteland of financial hardships so you will see Him as your Great Provider? Is He allowing you a journey through parched areas of loss so you will see Him as your Greatest Possession?

When we filter our circumstances through the grid of His unfailing love, we will see every test and trial, every desert and disappointment, as a loving gesture on His part to draw us closer to Himself. We will hear His gentle whisper, "I have drawn you with lovingkindness" (Jeremiah 31:3 NASB).

When we love God perfectly, we will trust Him implicitly. And where there is absolute trust, there is no fear.

*Lord, help me to trust You in the deserts of my life,
knowing You are pulling me closer to Yourself.*

Choosing to Rejoice

This is the day which the LORD has
made; let us rejoice and be glad in it.

PSALM 118:24 NASB

Holly knows what it's like to have one of those days that you wish you could do over. It started at 4:30 a.m., when she opened the door of her house to pick up the newspaper she thought was on the mat and...*thunk!* The newspaper delivery boy unknowingly chucked that newspaper through the early morning still-dark air and it pelted her right in the chest. *Nice aim,* she thought sarcastically. And she went inside and closed the door.

The rest of the day didn't get much better. Yet Holly kept her sense of humor and laughed about it with me and several women in our exercise class at the end of the day.

We all have days when we get pelted with something. A stinging insult. An unexpected action by a coworker. News that causes us to double over. Yet God told us how to handle it. "Rejoice...[and] again I will say, rejoice" (Philippians 4:4 NASB)

Lord, I will rejoice in this day that You have given me
simply because You have told me to.

It's No Accident

No purpose of Yours can be thwarted.

JOB 42:2 NASB

Shirley tried to keep her perspective amidst her disappointment. Her trip to Cancun the next morning with her daughter wouldn't be taking place now that she lay in a hospital bed, still grappling with the reality of a stroke she had several hours earlier.

"Why did this have to happen *now*?" she asked, knowing there wouldn't be an answer in the room that day. The Answer was still working out the details of a situation that never took Him by surprise. I wonder if He was whispering to her, sweetly, "All the days ordained for [you] were written in [My] book before one of them came to be" (Psalm 139:16).

Shirley had cleaned her house, packed her bags, and made arrangements for her dog to be cared for before she found herself in the hospital. God knew she was going to be leaving her home for a while...just not to go to the place *she* had planned.

Lord, I trust You with how this day turns out, even if it's not what I planned. I'm comforted knowing there is no accident when it comes to You.

Second-Guessing God

We know that God causes all things
to work together for good
to those who love God, to those who are
called according to His purpose.

ROMANS 8:28 NASB

How often do we ask God, "Why now?" "Why this?" "Why me?"

And yet God knows what He is doing. He has reasons far above our own because He is God and we are not. And we are asked to simply trust:

- That "there is an appointed time for everything" (Ecclesiastes 3:1 NASB) and that means He didn't get the timing wrong in the slightest.
- That "his works are perfect" (Deuteronomy 32:4) and He is a God who never makes mistakes.
- That He is a God who neither slumbers nor sleeps (Psalm 121:3-4), meaning *nothing* takes Him by surprise.

Lord, I will trust You even when it seems like my world is turning upside down. I know You are in control, and—because You are loving and good—You wouldn't have things any other way.

Keep Talking to Jesus

Pray without ceasing.

1 THESSALONIANS 5:17 NASB

Monica had just a few miles to go. An experienced marathon runner, she knew she could scale another hill. *If Jesus could endure the cross for me, I can run up this hill for Him,* she thought.

"Help me, Jesus; I'm doing this for You," she said aloud, repeatedly, as she continued the race. But paramedics stopped her at the top of the hill. They made her sit down, checked her pulse, and offered her fluids. They asked if she was all right and said they were told by other runners that she was delirious, probably dehydrated, and talking to herself.

"I'm fine. I was talking to *Jesus*!" she exclaimed, and insisted on continuing the race. Whether she's competing or training to stay in shape, Monica continues to pray aloud while running—regardless of who hears.

Lord, You are the One who strengthens me for all tasks. Help me to keep talking to You today, whether I need strength, encouragement, or just want to tell You that I love You. The world won't understand. But I know You will be smiling.

He Will Carry You

*He knows our frame; He
remembers that we are dust.*

PSALM 103:14 NKJV

Nancy wasn't prepared for the steep uphill climbs on her grueling 40-mile bicycle ride. Her friend, Rick, offered support by driving ahead of her, then coming back and telling her what was around the next corner. But each time Nancy started up a hill again, she struggled. After driving back down another time to tell her what lay ahead, Rick stopped, got out, picked up Nancy's bike, and put it in the back of his truck. Then he drove her up the hill, stopped, lifted her bike out of the truck, and put it back on the ground for her to resume her ride. "He did that over and over again and never said a word. That was grace," Nancy recalls.

When we struggle, we are often determined to pedal harder and wear ourselves out getting through it. But God knows what is around the next bend. Instead of shouting, "Come on, pedal harder!" God quietly *carries* us up those hills.

Lord, You know what lies ahead, and I praise You for being the One who carries me uphill.

He Knows

O LORD, You have searched me and known me.

PSALM 139:1 NASB

Carrie remembers feeling anxious as her husband drove her to the hospital for the tests. She was about to discover that she had a heart defect she had been born with, and that heart surgery was inevitable.

On the way to her appointment, she pulled out her Bible and read Psalm 139. In the New Living Translation (which she happened to have in the car with her that morning), the first verse read, "O LORD, you have examined my heart and know everything about me."

"The God who created me, who knows every cell in my being, reached down to let me know that He has *examined my heart.* He knows...and He cares," Carrie said.

Lord, I praise You that I too have Someone who is intimately acquainted with all the details of my life. I have Someone who is capable of getting me through whatever lies ahead. Thank You for knowing my history, my health, my heart, and my happenings from day to day.

Your Right-Hand Man

I have set the LORD continually before me;
because he is at my right hand, I will not be shaken.

PSALM 16:8 NASB

I remember the day I felt like I was losing my right hand. A woman I depended on to be my sounding board and my prayer support informed me she needed to be moving on from my church. I suddenly felt "cut off." Hours earlier, I had spoken to a group of women on the seasons of our life in which we need to be pruned. But here I was, being pruned in my own life, and feeling like I was losing my right hand!

Desperate for God's presence and His comfort, I turned to Psalm 16 and read it aloud. I stopped suddenly at verse 8: "Because *he* is at my right hand, I will not be shaken."

Lord, on those days that I feel cut off from help, encouragement, or support, help me remember that You are the One who is at my right hand. You are the One who helps me, counsels me, encourages me. Because of Your stability, I will never be shaken.

Joy in His Presence

You make known to me the path of life;
you will fill me with joy in your presence,
with eternal pleasures at your right hand.

PSALM 16:11

During a season of loss, it's natural to believe we will never experience joy again. But seasons of loss can remind us that what we lost was not our container of joy. Joy exists in the presence of the One who will never leave. The One who remains at our side. The One who holds eternal pleasures in His right hand.

If you are anxious about feeling alone, realize you never will be. Your Right-Hand Man is at your side, and there is joy in His presence. Is there anyone else you would rather have at your side? Walk today with your head held high and your Right-Hand Man at your side. You have never yet walked alone. And you never will.

Lord, thank You for the gentle reminder in Your Word that I never walk alone. You are always at my side. I'm ready to experience joy in Your presence, and I'm looking forward to the "eternal pleasures" at Your right hand.

Lighten Your Load

Come to me, all you who are weary and
burdened, and I will give you rest.

MATTHEW 11:28

A re you feeling today that there is *too much* to do?
I remember a time in my life when I felt like I was
drowning under my obligations. There was so much
to do to keep up with family relationships, to keep up
the house, to keep up with my job and ministry, and
to keep up in my walk with God. I felt I was continually coming up short. And it was weighing me down.

I truly believe that when we feel like that it's because
we are taking on more than God intended us to bear.
He is God and we are not. And He is the God of Rest,
not the God of Perpetual Stress! How do you need to
lighten your load and trust God with the rest?

Lord, I give You all that weighs me down today. Help
me to see the few things You have called me to do. Help
me then to do my best, and trust You with the rest.

He Provides Rest

Take my yoke upon you and learn from me,
for I am gentle and humble in heart,
and you will find rest for your souls.

MATTHEW 11:29

What is burdening you today? A relationship? A financial situation? A problem you feel you can't solve? If you are feeling burdened, chances are you are carrying far more than Your heavenly Father intended for you to bear.

The heaviest load He has placed on us is to love Him with all our hearts. That load is easy and that burden is light. Leave the other burdens at His feet. He is capable of working out all that is on your heart and mind and leaving you with shoulders that feel light and free.

Lord Jesus, You are ever aware of the burdens that are placed on me by others and those that I take on myself. Yet, when I consider loving You as my highest obligation, all the other things I think I have to do pale in comparison. There is anxiety and stress in striving to carry my own burdens. There is peace and rest in loving You.

He's Always Listening

I call out to the LORD, and he answers
me from his holy mountain.

PSALM 3:4

Who do *you* call first when there's something on your heart and mind that you need to share? I've learned from experience that if I go to someone else, I'm eventually going to be disappointed—by their unavailability, their response, or their lack of response. David said when he cried out to God, "He answers." Did you catch that? God isn't on another call. He isn't too busy to hear your call. He isn't distracted by another incoming call. *He answers.*

As you go through this day, tell God first about all that comes your way. Of course, He already knows what you're about to say. But by telling *Him* your news first, you're affirming to Him—and yourself—that He is the most important One in your life. And you have a guarantee that He's listening.

Thank You, Lord, that while others don't have time or don't realize the importance of what I need to say, You are always there. Remind me that You are my Greatest Encourager, my Greatest Support, my Ever-Present Counselor and Help.

A Steep Climb

*After six days Jesus took Peter, James and John
with him and led them up a high
mountain, where they were all alone.
There he was transfigured before them.*

MARK 9:2

Just a little further," my husband said to me as we continued the long, steep climb up Double Peak. The last 100-foot stretch was nearly a straight-up climb. I was huffing and puffing…and vowing never to do something like this again. But by the time I reached the top, my husband took my hand and walked me to where I could see over the edge. There beneath me was a breathtaking panoramic view of not only the town where we live, but the neighboring cities on either side, with a view stretching westward to the Pacific Ocean. It was a beautiful, clear morning. And my husband knew what I would experience at the top if I just kept going.

Lord, there are times I complain about the "uphill climbs" in my life. But You know what is awaiting me at the top. I trust You, Lord, even when the climb is difficult.

Beholding His Glory

*After six days Jesus took Peter, James and John
with him and led them up a high mountain…
There he was transfigured before them.*

MARK 9:2

I wonder if Jesus' disciples felt the same way I did as
they were climbing up a steep mountain. I wonder
if they started to grumble to themselves as they went
through the switchbacks, tired and out of breath. But
Jesus knew what they would experience if they just kept
going.

I imagine in those moments as they were catching
their breath that Peter wanted to say, "What *now*? What
are we supposed to do up here? And once we get to the
top, we'll have to go all the way back down again too!"
But once they arrived at their destination with Jesus,
they saw Him in all His glory. Immediately, Jesus' disciples knew the experience was worth the climb.

*Lord, I too want to see You more fully. Take me to a
place where I can experience Your glory no matter
what we go through on the way.*

Worth the Climb

Jesus...led them up a high mountain...
There he was transfigured before them.

MARK 9:2

Where has God been taking *you* lately? Up a steep hill? Through a dry, parched desert? On a perilous journey? Are you at the place where you're saying, "What now, Lord? Is this all there is?" Or maybe you're thinking, *This is uncomfortable. I wasn't planning on it being like this. Can we turn back now?* But Jesus clearly knows what you're about to experience...if you continue with Him to the place where He wants to take you.

If God has asked you to follow Him up a steep climb or on a traverse path, hold tight, my friend. Perhaps Jesus wants to show you something of His glory. Or maybe He wants to transform *you* before *His* eyes. One thing is for sure: You're in for a great adventure.

Lord, help me to trust You on the uphill journeys, knowing that You are going before Me. I truly want to see what You have in store for me and I look forward to seeing how You will transform me as well.

Waiting on Him

My soul, wait silently for God alone,
for my expectation is from Him.

PSALM 62:5 NKJV

What is it you are waiting on God for? A plan? A purpose? A dream? A desire? Healing? Hope? Many times God asks us to wait on Him because there is something more He wants to do in us as we wait. Trust that there is a reason for the waiting. And then—in quiet confidence—know that when the time comes and that door opens, He will be going through it with you.

God, thank You that You already know what lies ahead of me. So there is wisdom in Your instruction to wait. Sometimes I have no choice but to wait because things don't move along as quickly as I'd like. But help me to remember that when I find myself waiting it's because Your love is holding me at bay so I can learn what I need to know in order to go through that next door. I am confident that when I do, You will be right beside me.

Waiting for Him

*Wait for the LORD; be strong and take
heart and wait for the LORD.*

PSALM 27:14

Have you ever wondered what it is you're supposed
to be waiting for when we're told in Scripture to wait
on the Lord? Are we waiting for an answer? Waiting for
direction? Waiting for a green light to finally proceed
with what we've been waiting to do? Perhaps we are
being told to simply wait *for Him*. We wait for *Him* to
develop our faith. We wait for *Him* to transform us in
the waiting process. We wait for *His* direction and *His*
straightening out of our path.

*Lord, why would I ever want to run out ahead of
You and into things by myself? There is wisdom in
waiting—waiting for the One who has walked with
me through my yesterdays and has already walked
ahead of me into my tomorrows. Remind me, Lord,
that I wait not for an answer or a direction or a
circumstance. I am waiting for You—the Answer, the
Direction, and the God of My Circumstances.*

He Delights in You

He brought me out into a spacious place;
he rescued me because he delighted in me.

Psalm 18:19

When David cried out to God in Psalm 18 to be rescued from his enemies, God brought him to a "spacious place."

Are the enemies of busyness, stress, and fatigue pressing in on you? Do you feel the pressure to work harder, run faster, achieve more, only to be exhausted? Then perhaps you are in need of a rescue by the God of Rest, who is longing to bring you out into a spacious place. Or perhaps He has already. If you are finding yourself in a lonely place right now with not much going on, not many friends around, not much hope in front of you…look more closely. God just may have already brought you to a spacious place that you haven't yet realized is your rescue. Drink deeply of that space, my friend. And meet there with the One who has come to your rescue.

Rescue me, Lord Jesus, from the busyness of this life.
And bring me to the spacious place of Your embrace.

He Knows Your Heart

To You they cried out and were delivered;
in You they trusted and were not disappointed.

PSALM 22:5 NASB

Are there people in your life you continue to disappoint? Do you get frustrated at the thought that there are too many people to please and too little of you? Are you sometimes ready to quit because you can't seem to get it right when it comes to relationships? Take heart, my friend. There is One who knows your heart and your hurts, your intentions and your oversights, your disappointments and your frustrations. He knows all about you and continues to love you just the same. Hope in Him. Pour out your heart to Him. And let Him be the One to clear your name.

Lord, thank You that You know me more than any other. May You be the One I run to when I am frustrated from disappointing yet another person. Thank You that even though I have disappointed You many times, You still call me friend.

Filling Your Heart with Songs

He put a new song in my mouth,
a hymn of praise to our God.

PSALM 40:3

Alice lay on the cold exam table as she was moved into the tube-like chamber. She was undergoing an MRI of her brain to determine why she was experiencing loss of balance. At first she kept her eyes open when the hood enclosed her, but then she realized she needed to close her eyes and turn her thoughts to something else. All sorts of sounds were emitting from the machine. A crashing sound, some pinging. Noises here and there. As she kept her eyes shut and tried to relax, she began to put the sounds together and make a song. Alice was creating a symphony of praise in the midst of her uncertainty.

No matter where we are—on the exam table, in a hospital waiting room, alone on a plane, sitting by the phone—He can fill us with songs.

Lord, "put a new song in my mouth" today. Regardless of what happens, I don't want to miss Your whispers of love through the songs You send my way.

He Gives Songs in the Night

By day the LORD directs his love,
at night his song is with me.

PSALM 42:8

My daughter called from her college dorm room. Her heart had been broken and she couldn't sleep. I gave Dana some verses that would comfort her heart and help her get through the night.

"I like the one about Him giving us songs," Dana texted later, referring to Psalm 119:54: "No matter where I am, your teachings fill me with songs" (CEV). As soon as Dana could speak, I taught her to sing about whatever she was experiencing. If she was tired, we'd sing about it. If she was hungry, we'd sing. If she was sad, we found a song. Singing kept her heart light and focused not on the situation, but on the song. It was a way of distracting her from worry or uncertainty and causing her to keep a song—and some joy—in her heart.

God, You are the One "who gives songs in the night"
(Job 35:10) to comfort or distract me from distress.
Thank You for whispering to me—and those I love—
through Your songs.

Listen for Your Song

He will quiet you with His love,
He will rejoice over you with singing.

Zephaniah 3:17 nkjv

Are you facing uncertainty today? When you focus your mind on Him, He has a way of helping you pull together the sounds and situations of your life into a symphony of praise to Him.

On those days when a song comes to our hearts, I wonder if it is *God's song* over us that we hear. Zephaniah 3:17 says, "He celebrates and sings because of you" (cev). God sings over us, and we ought to sing over Him, over our circumstances, over anything that might cause us to feel lonely or scared. Next time you start to worry, listen for your song—it could be *Him* singing over *you.*

Jesus, You are the Giver of songs. The next time I feel afraid, lonely, or worried, fill my heart with a song for You—something simple, yet serene, that will flood my mind with peace and my heart with joy. For all the times You've sung over me, I want to start singing over You.

Finding Your Quiet Retreat

You're my place of quiet retreat;
I wait for your Word to renew me.

PSALM 119:114 MSG

I remember waking up one morning and thinking, *I don't feel like facing this day.* I dragged myself to the Psalms because I had nowhere else to go. In those songs of Scripture, I sensed the heartbreak, the happiness, the frustration, the elation, and the desperation of human songwriters filled with emotions just like mine. And there in Scripture's songs I discovered a pattern. In all 150 of the Psalms, the phrase "I will" was sung 140 times. Despite how the songwriters *felt*, there were certain things they were determined to *do*. And I realized that there were certain things I needed to say "I will" about, too, starting with the one phrase that has changed my life through the years: "I *will* not neglect your word" (Psalm 119:16).

> *Lord, may Your Word be my morning motivation and the quiet retreat to which I return at the end of every day.*

Your Island Hideaway

GOD's my island hideaway,
keeps danger far from the shore,
throws garlands of hosannas around my neck.

PSALM 32:7 MSG

Is life taking its toll on you? Do you need a "hiding place" to which you can go and be renewed and refreshed?

Let God be your place of quiet retreat—that tower of refuge to which you can run, that shelter in which you can hide away with Him and His Word and listen to what He wants to say to you in the pages of His book. It is there that you can be refreshed, renewed, and reminded of the One who's been waiting to get away with you.

God, help me to realize that I can get away with You in my heart anytime by finding a quiet place and opening Your Word. Take me to the strong tower in Your Word where I can find refuge, the green pastures of Your Word where You can feed my soul, and the spacious places in Your Word where I can find rest.

All Day Long

My mouth will tell of your righteous deeds,
of your saving acts all day long.

PSALM 71:15

Is your mind remembering and your mouth recounting His righteousness all day long? Sometimes, in order to keep telling of His goodness, we must remember the pit He pulled us out of or where we would so easily be today had His tender mercies not intervened. And while we may think our salvation story is an old one that others are tired of hearing, we have new stories every day of His "saving acts" if we would open our eyes and look all around at how He is moving in our lives.

What do you need saving from today? An old, persistent habit? Negative or destructive thoughts? Past baggage that is still affecting you? A critical spirit? A tendency to live for yourself and miss the joy of serving someone else?

Lord, save me from myself—and all that keeps me from glorifying You—today. I will praise Your name continually by telling of Your saving acts from sunrise to sunset.

He Demonstrated His Love

God demonstrates his own love for us in this:
While we were still sinners, Christ died for us.

ROMANS 5:8

For years, Jean endured a loveless marriage and wondered at times if God really loved her too. Because she was looking for something tangible and emotional, she continued to feel unloved and alone. Then one day Jean's friend showed her the facts from Scripture about God's love for her:

- God loved us so much He sent His Son to die in our place (1 John 4:10).
- There is nowhere we can go where His presence is not with us (Psalm 139:7-11).
- Nothing can separate us from the love of God (Romans 8:38-39).

Sometimes, like Jean, we don't *feel* God's love either. But those are the times we need to rely on the facts rather than our feelings.

Lord, You have said that without faith it is impossible to please You. On days when I don't feel loved, help me to exercise faith by remembering the facts about what You have done on my behalf.

Slow Down

He stilled the storm to a whisper;
the waves of the sea were hushed.

PSALM 107:29

Anita was running late again. She headed down some side streets to avoid traffic and get to her destination more quickly. Suddenly she realized she must have made a wrong turn. She was on a narrow one-way road that didn't appear to be leading anywhere. *Lord, I don't have time to get lost*, she began to pray. That's when she noticed the sign, large and bright, ahead of her: SLOW. *Oh great—there must be some construction taking place here*, she thought. But then she came upon another sign, this one blinking, so she wouldn't miss it: S-L-O-W. *Oh, no, Lord, I'm not going to make it in time... what are You trying to tell me?* The next sign flashed scrolling words: S-L-O-W D-O-W-N. *I get it, God*, she said softly.

Thank You, Lord, for the times You arrange even the traffic patterns to whisper—or shout—what it is You want me to hear. Help me to slow down and listen.

A New Song

I waited patiently for the LORD;
he turned to me and heard my cry.
He lifted me out of the slimy pit,
out of the mud and mire;
he set my feet on a rock
and gave me a firm place to stand.
He put a new song in my mouth,
a hymn of praise to our God.

PSALM 40:1-3

Do you know what it's like to have God put a new song in your mouth? It happens when you let Him pull you out of the pit.

What is the slimy pit from which *you* need God to deliver you? An unhealthy habit? A strong addiction? A destructive relationship? Those things are difficult to release when we want to hold onto them tightly. But when we surrender and ask God to replace our destructive desires with a desperation for Himself, that is a prayer He hears and heeds. Then we will find ourselves on solid rock, with a new song to sing.

Lord, pull me out of the pit that is keeping me from glorifying You. And I will sing of Your rescue.

Immeasurably More

Now to Him who is able to do
immeasurably more
than all we ask or imagine,
according to his power that is at work within us...

EPHESIANS 3:20

Are you settling for less? Do you know that you can do better in your dating relationship or your job or your present circumstance, but you just don't have the strength to make the change or the faith to ask God for more?

Scripture says God can do "immeasurably more than all we ask or imagine." That means we don't imagine big enough to ask God for what He's really capable of.

Listen to Him whispering the "immeasurably more" into your ear. Whether it be something unhealthy that's plaguing you or a job that is sucking the life out of you, you could be settling for second choice when God has first choice waiting for you in the wings.

God, don't let me settle for what I think You can do.
Expand my faith to ask for what You really can do in
my life. I want Your best for me, not what I'm afraid
to live without.

He Can Do Anything

God can do anything, you know—
far more than you could ever imagine or
guess or request in your wildest dreams!

EPHESIANS 3:20 MSG

How big is your God? You answer that question by what you are *willing* to accept and what you are *unwilling* to expect. The God who numbers the hairs on your head, saves your tears in a bottle, and has thoughts of you too numerable to mention wants to blow your expectations out of the water by coming through in a mighty way for you. The problem is we tend to ask God for just what we think He is capable of, not for the "immeasurably more" that He is dying to accomplish in our lives. And yet "is anything too difficult for the LORD?" (Genesis 18:14 NASB). Listen for the affirming whispers of the One who can do *anything*.

Lord, I want Your first choice, not the consolation prize
for a woman too hesitant to ask You for more. May I
thrill Your heart by believing You for great things.

His Whispers of Protection

No good thing will He withhold
from those who walk uprightly.

PSALM 84:11 NKJV

In my Bible, Psalm 84:11 is highlighted. I claimed this promise as I asked God for Hugh to become my husband. Hugh was the godly man who had stolen my heart.

"Hugh is a good thing for me, God," I prayed. "Certainly You will not withhold him from me." And God didn't. A year after praying that promise, Hugh and I were married, and I can confirm that over the past 25 years, Hugh has been a "good thing" in my life.

Yet there are other "good things" I have prayed for through the years that God has chosen to withhold: a second child, a different home, a dream job. God, in His wisdom and love, knows what He is protecting us from when He withholds something that looks truly good to us.

Lord, I thank You for the times You have blessed me
with what I want. And I trust You with the times that
You withhold things for my good. Thank You for Your
whispers of protection through what You withhold.

Something Better Awaits

So we fix our eyes not on what is seen,
but on what is unseen,
since what is seen is temporary,
but what is unseen is eternal.

2 Corinthians 4:18

When my cousin, Mark, slipped into a coma and then left this earth, I realized how much I longed to be home—in that place where there will be no more death or tears or fears. Where there will be eternal joy in God's presence.

I won't see Mark again until my life on this earth is over. My sense of loss leads to a longing for the place where I will never have to experience any kind of loss again.

We all have days when we don't want to be here anymore. The reasons abound: the loss of a loved one. Divorce. Deteriorating health. Unbearable pain. Crushed dreams. But there is hope for those of us who know Jesus personally. This life is not the end-all. Something far better awaits.

Lord, through death and loss, I hear Your gentle whispers reminding me that this world is not my home. Thank You that something far better awaits.

His Will for Us

Give thanks in all circumstances;
for this is God's will for you in Christ Jesus.

1 THESSALONIANS 5:18

God desires that we be people who can give thanks "in all circumstances"—even the bad ones—because He knows that the ability to rejoice in the tough times is God-given. It's an act of obedience that shapes us and reminds us that life is not just about us and our comfort and convenience, but about the One who made us and is worthy of our praise.

In all things, give thanks. Or, *in all things, sing.* Why? Because anyone—whether they know God or not—can be thankful in the good things. But it takes a person of obedience and surrender to praise God in the pain and to sing in the suffering. In all things, sing. And as you do, you will be living out His will for you.

God, help me to be thankful in all things, and to constantly hear Your whispers of love reminding me that as long as I have You, I have all I need.

Strength for the Weary

My soul melts from heaviness;
strengthen me according to Your word.

PSALM 119:28 NKJV

Do you know what it's like to feel that "heaviness"? Sometimes we're not even sure where it's coming from. But God understands completely the concerns that weigh you down. The psalmist looked to Scripture to strengthen his weary soul. And there, we too can find what we need to alleviate the heaviness. In Psalm 119, we find that God's Word...

- counsels us and gives us direction (verses 24,105)
- liberates us so that we truly feel free (verses 32,45)
- brings us delight (verses 35,111)
- focuses us on what matters (verse 37)
- comforts us in our suffering (verse 50)
- inspires us and gives us perspective (verse 54)
- sustains us and prolongs our hope (verse 116)

O God, You understand the source of my heaviness. And You are my Source of Strength. Thank You for the preserving power of Your Word.

Refreshment from His Word

The law of the LORD is perfect, refreshing the soul.
The statutes of the LORD are trustworthy,
making wise the simple.
The precepts of the LORD are right,
giving joy to the heart.
The commands of the LORD are radiant,
giving light to the eyes.

PSALM 19:7-8

Could you use some refreshment today? Would you like added wisdom, joy, and enlightenment too? Look again at David's song that describes what Scripture can do for your tired, worn-out soul. If something were available to you that revives you, gives you wisdom, brings joy to your heart, and brightens your eyes—all in one drink or pill—wouldn't you want to take it on a daily basis? You *can* have revival, wisdom, joy, and enlightenment—every day—by opening up God's Word and drinking it in like a daily dose of vitamins for your mind, body, and soul.

Lord, increase my desire for Your Word, and help me to turn to it when I need Your refreshment, wisdom, enlightenment, and joy.

A Breath of Fresh Air

All Scripture is God-breathed
and is useful for teaching,
rebuking, correcting and training in righteousness.

2 TIMOTHY 3:16

Feeling like you could use a second wind this morning? God whispers—and refuels us—through His Word. The New Testament writer told us "all Scripture is *God-breathed*." Think about that. Reading the Bible is like getting a *breath of fresh air* from the living God! It's like getting a second wind—from God—that teaches us, rebukes us, corrects us, and trains us in righteousness so we can be "thoroughly equipped for every good work" (verse 17). That doesn't just mean so we can be thoroughly equipped to teach Sunday school or lead a ministry or be an approved theologian. It means we'll be thoroughly equipped for *every good work*…for all the things you need to do today as a woman, a wife, a daughter, a mother, an employee, a supervisor, or a friend.

Lord, thank You for the breath of fresh air that You give me through Your Word. Help me to listen for Your gentle whispers, through Your Word, to get me through the day.

Good to Be Near Him

As for me, it is good to be near God.
I have made the Sovereign LORD my refuge;
I will tell of all your deeds.

PSALM 73:28

It is good for some to be near money so they won't worry about their provision. It is good for some to be near hope so they don't slip into despair. It is good for some to be near activity, so they don't have to face the questions that burden their hearts when all is quiet. And it is good for some to be near people so they don't feel the ache of loneliness. But as for me, it is good to be near God. When I am with Him, and not all that keeps me in perfect comfort, it is then that I can grow in faith, and "without faith it is impossible to please God" (Hebrews 11:6).

Lord, may I find my security, hope, purpose, and companionship in You. May I make the Sovereign Lord my refuge so that, as I am near You, I can hear You whispering, "You are never alone."

His Shepherding Heart

The LORD is my shepherd, I lack nothing.

PSALM 23:1

When David talked of his Good Shepherd in Psalm 23, he described the ways God provided for him—physically, emotionally, and spiritually.

Listen to the description of *your* Good and Loving Shepherd:

- *He makes me lie down in green pastures.* He knows when His sheep *need* to rest, but won't. So He has a way of leading us toward certain *green pastures* and then *making* us lie down. How has He *made* you rest in "green pastures"?

- *He leads me beside quiet waters.* Not along the frantic freeway or down the busy block, but near the *quiet waters.* Have you experienced the quiet waters of His Word, His ways, His whispers?

- *He refreshes my soul.* Leave it to God to know when and how we need to be refreshed, and to provide those opportunities for us every day.

Lord, open my eyes to notice the green pastures, the quiet waters, and the refreshment that You faithfully send my way.

Tough and Tender

See, the Sovereign LORD comes with power, and
he rules with a mighty arm. See, his reward is
with him, and his recompense accompanies him.
He tends his flock like a shepherd: He gathers
the lambs in his arms and carries them close to
his heart; he gently leads those that have young.

ISAIAH 40:10-11

God is sovereign and rules with a mighty arm. And
yet He uses those same arms to gather together His
lambs and hold them close to His heart. God is the
One who judges. And yet He is also the One who gently leads "the nursing ewes" (NASB). He ascends "amid
shouts of joy" and blaring trumpets (Psalm 47:5), yet
He speaks to His beloved through a "gentle whisper"
(1 Kings 19:12).

Mighty God, I love that You are both tough and tender.
You rule with authority and execute justice, yet You
heal the brokenhearted and bind up their wounds
(Psalm 147:3). May I never lose sight of the fact that
You are the Everlasting, All-Powerful Lord. And yet
may I rejoice upon remembering that, in spite of Your
power, You see me as precious.

He Never Tires

Do you not know? Have you not heard?
The Lord is the everlasting God,
the Creator of the ends of the earth.
He will not grow tired or weary, and his
understanding no one can fathom.
He gives strength to the weary and
increases the power of the weak.

Isaiah 40:28-29

At nearly 50 years of age, I'm finding there are days when I don't move as well as I used to. And after exercising four days straight, I'm a little tired when I start my workout on the fifth day of the week. But imagine this! We worship—and wait upon—a God who is from everlasting to everlasting and *never* grows tired or weary of us. Even those who are younger grow tired and weary at times, as implied by Isaiah 40:30. But God is the One who continues to offer us strength and renewal and understanding that no one can fathom.

Lord, to whom else can I go? To whom else would I ever want to go? Thank You for offering to me—the weak—Your incredible strength.

Strength to Soar

Those who hope in the LORD
will renew their strength.
They will soar on wings like eagles;
they will run and not grow weary,
they will walk and not be faint.

ISAIAH 40:31

Are you in need of renewed strength today? Would you like to know what it is to soar? Scripture says you can have that strength when you "wait for the LORD" (NASB). I'm so glad the prophet Isaiah didn't say that "those who try their best and work harder will find more energy to keep plowing forward." Scripture says as we wait—not run faster—we will find new strength and "soar on wings like eagles." Have you ever seen eagles soar? It all appears so effortless and majestic. That's the kind of soaring we will do when we *wait* upon God to renew our strength, and when we hope in Him for our renewal.

Lord, I'm ready to soar on eagles' wings. I'm ready to run and not grow weary, and to walk without fainting. Be my Source of Strength, the whisper in my ear, and the wind beneath my wings.

For His Name's Sake

*For your name's sake, L*ORD*, preserve my life;*
in your righteousness, bring me out of trouble.

Have you considered that what becomes of you reflects upon God's name and reputation? He has drawn us to Himself and called us His own so that what happens to us is directly associated with His character, His goodness, and His love. That should give you great assurance, knowing that God will be true to His character in whatever He allows to happen to you. He is the God who chooses to be glorified in us so we can rest assured that He will also take care of His own. Are you seeking refuge in Him? Then in His righteousness and for the sake of His name, He will bring you out of trouble.

Thank You, God, that in upholding Your name and reputation, You will be upholding me as well. In Your righteousness, be pleased to bring me out of trouble so You will be revered.

For His Fame

You are my rock and my fortress,
for the sake of your name lead and guide me.

Your dreams and your destiny are just as important to God as they are to you. Listen to His whispers concerning you: "I know the plans I have for you...plans to prosper you and not to harm you, plans to give you hope and a future" (Jeremiah 29:11).

God not only desires the best for you, but His name and reputation are at stake in what ultimately becomes of you. If you begin to see your life in terms of what God wants in order to glorify Himself, you won't worry when your plans fall through. You will, instead, anticipate what great things He has coming. When God's fame is the prayer on your heart, God can do "immeasurably more than all we ask or imagine" (Ephesians 3:20).

Lord, how can I worry about my destiny if my life is in Your hands? Ultimately what becomes of me reflects upon Your name. So have Your way with me for the sake of Your glory and fame.

Never Out of His Sight

The LORD is your protector, and he
won't go to sleep or let you stumble.

PSALM 121:3 CEV

Can you fathom the idea of someone caring for you every moment of the day, every minute that you sleep, wherever you go, whatever you do—watching you and protecting you?

That is what God does. Perhaps the idea of someone following you everywhere, tracking your every move, never taking his eyes off of you would make you uncomfortable. Yet when it's the God of the Universe—whose loving-kindness is from everlasting to everlasting and who never lets you out of His sight—that should be not only comforting, but mind-blowing! There is nowhere you can go where He is not watching, no way to lose Him. He is obsessed with you. He sticks to you like glue.

Next time you begin to feel alone, remember that you have a Bodyguard going into every situation with you and—carefully, lovingly, and expertly—guiding you home.

Thank You, God, that I am guarded by the One who never slumbers nor sleeps, nor will let my foot slip.

Chosen by His Love

You did not choose me, but I chose you.

JOHN 15:16

I used to think I had made a great decision as a young child to follow Jesus. *Smart kid that I was*, I thought. But it was no doing of my own. It was *His* love that drew me; *His* grace that chose me. And the more I live life, and the more I look at God's Word, the more convinced I am of that.

Where were *you* when God's loving-kindness began to call? What were you doing when He began to draw you toward Himself? Have you thanked Him today for intervening in your life in the way that He has so that He can call you His own? Think about it: Where would you be were it not for His love?

Lord Jesus, thank You for crashing into my world and finding a way to make me Your own. When I begin to feel unworthy, unnoticed, or unloved, remind me that the God of the Universe called me by name and drew me to Himself. That is amazing love. And that love is mine.

Desiring Nothing Else

Whom have I in heaven but You?
And there is none upon earth
that I desire besides You.

PSALM 73:25 NKJV

I first copied this verse onto a note card and put it on my refrigerator more than 20 years ago. I was comforted by the truth that I have an Advocate in heaven, and He is *mine*.

Whom do I have but You, God? It is more than a question or even a statement. It is a motto. And I have reminded myself to live by that motto ever since. Only *You*, Lord, are perfect. Only *You* are incapable of disappointing me. Only *You* can satisfy.

As long as we are hoping for lasting fulfillment through intimacy with a person on this earth, we will be disappointed. All are mere men. All have sinned. And all will let us down at one time or another.

Lord, whom have I in heaven but You? And I desire nothing on earth besides You. Make this the prayer of my heart so I will find that I already have all that I desire.

One Thing

One thing I ask from the LORD,
this only do I seek…
to gaze on the beauty of the LORD
and to seek him in his temple.

PSALM 27:4

Have you ever asked the Lord to change your husband—or just give you one?

I have.

"Please change his heart, Lord," I would pray. "Give him the ability to express himself to me in a way that fills my heart's hunger." But God wanted to change *my* heart instead, and He wanted to be the One to satisfy the hunger.

"Seek Me like my servant David did," God seemed to be saying to me through His Word. "Only I can fill your heart's hunger."

I realized that if David—who was described in Scripture as a man after God's own heart—wanted only one thing and that one thing was intimacy with God, I too had to want God above all else.

Lord, be the Husband I seek. Fill the longings of my heart with You alone so that I can truly say, "There is one thing I want, and it's You."

My Debt Erased

Jesus said, "It is finished."
JOHN 19:30

As I walked out the courtroom door I felt a sense of relief. I paid my fine for running the red light, and I was free to go. *It's over.* But it wasn't, really. The violation would still go on my driving record, causing my insurance rates to increase. And I would live for the next three years with the consequences of my offense. For a brief moment I thought about how nice it would be if that red-light violation—and the speeding ticket two months earlier—had never occurred. *I wish I could just erase that whole thing.*

It was then that God whispered to my heart, "I already have."

God wasn't referring to the traffic offense, but a much larger offense that was taken care of on my behalf. Jesus paid a huge debt I could *never* pay. And because of Him, my life's slate is clean.

Lord, I was a multiple offender, according to Your law. But by Your grace and Jesus' death for me, I am now innocent. Thank You.

So Walk in Him

*As you have received Christ Jesus
the Lord, so walk in Him.*

COLOSSIANS 2:6 NASB

Those are four simple words that are not so simple to live: "so walk in Him." Yet He is the One who gives us the strength to walk alongside Him obediently.

How do we walk in Him? "Walk by the Spirit, and you will not carry out the desire of the flesh" (Galatians 5:16 NASB).

As Paul wrote to the Colossians:

> My counsel for you is simple and straightforward: Just go ahead with what you've been given. You received Christ Jesus, the Master; now *live* him. You're deeply rooted in him. You're well constructed upon him. You know your way around the faith. Now do what you've been taught. School's out; quit studying the subject and start *living* it! And let your living spill over into thanksgiving (Colossians 2:6-7 MSG).

Lord, I need Your guiding and directing whispers to live this life You have called me to live.

Part III

Responding to His Heart

*Listen to His whispers on your
heart—and respond...*

Everywhere I Go

If I go up to the heavens, you are there;
if I make my bed in the depths, you are there.
If I rise on the wings of the dawn,
if I settle on the far side of the sea,
even there your hand will guide me,
your right hand will hold me fast.

PSALM 139:8-10

I am comforted, Lord, by Your staying power and Your amazing ability to track me everywhere I go. There is great security in knowing that there's no place I can go where You will not follow. There's no place I can seek out where Your presence is not already there. Nowhere to run, nowhere to hide—as if I'd ever want to. You follow me like a shadow. You stick to me like glue. Not only will You never leave, You will never let me out of Your sight.

Lord, I never want to run or hide. Instead, may I find comfort knowing there's nowhere I can go where Your pursuing love will not follow.

Drawn by Your Love

I have loved you with an everlasting love;
therefore I have drawn you with lovingkindness.

JEREMIAH 31:3 NASB

You, God, have loved us from everlasting to everlasting. You have drawn us toward Yourself. And even after we've gone after other loves, as Your people historically did, Your words to them echo into our hearts today: "[I] will call you back as if you were a wife deserted and distressed in spirit" (Isaiah 54:6).

Oh God, where would I be had You not drawn me toward Yourself? I'm so thankful that You didn't wait for me to decide to follow You. Your Word says, "There is no one who does good, not even one" (Romans 3:12), and I didn't have it in me to choose You first. So You extended Yourself toward me. On the days that I don't feel worthy of You, remind me, Lord Jesus, that it was You who drew me to Yourself. It was You who extended love first by sending Your only Son (1 John 4:10).

Doorkeeping for the Lord

I would rather be a doorkeeper
in the house of my God
than dwell in the tents of the wicked.

PSALM 84:10

Lord, at times it's easy to feel that people who don't honor You have it better than me. Yet David, a man who was promised the throne of Israel and had to wait years before You gave it to him, said he would rather hold a door open, as Your hired hand, than live richly apart from you. David was sleeping on the hard, rocky ground, and catching his own food, while King Saul was lying on comfortable pillows and eating whatever his heart desired. It didn't seem fair. Yet the rightful king said, in so many words, "I would rather live simply, and have God near, than have it *all* out there on my own."

I long to have the kind of heart that David had. I want to live simply, having You, rather than longing for what others have without You. I know that as I honor You, even during tough times when things don't seem fair, You will pull me close.

Your Higher Ways

"My thoughts are not your thoughts,
nor are your ways My ways," declares the LORD.

ISAIAH 55:8 NASB

How often I come to You, the Creator and Sustainer of Life, and ask, "Why?"

"Why *now*, God? Couldn't You have waited another week or so?"

"Why *her*, Lord? Couldn't you have let it happen to someone else?"

"Why *this*, God? Couldn't you have gotten my attention in some *other* way?"

And Your answer continues to remind me who is in control:

> As the heavens are higher than the earth,
>   so are My ways higher than your ways
>   and My thoughts than your thoughts
>   (Isaiah 55:9 NASB).

I love Your gentle way of telling me that Your plan is above and beyond anything that I can see here on earth...a story in a spiritual realm that I can't yet comprehend. I am asked to simply trust. You know best, and I can rest in that.

You Know Me Inside Out

Search me, O God, and know my heart;
try me and know my anxious thoughts.

PSALM 139:23 NASB

Lord, You have searched me and You know me. You know my thoughts before I think them, my words before I say them, and my actions before I carry them out. You know where I've been and where I'm headed (Psalm 139:1-4). You know the plans that You have for me, to give me a hope and a future (Jeremiah 29:11). You know every fiber of my being, every beat of my heart, every diagnosis that is yet to be made. You know the number of my days and the content in all of them. As the psalmist said, "Such knowledge is too wonderful for me" (Psalm 139:6). How can I not confidently place my life, my loved ones, and my longings in Your loving, capable hands? In light of what You know about me, may my response be like David's: "I have calmed and quieted myself, I am like a weaned child with its mother; like a weaned child I am content" (Psalm 131:2).

You Are My Refuge

Trust in him at all times, you people;
pour out your hearts to him, for God is our refuge.

Psalm 62:8

There are days when I need to pour out my heart but I'm not sure how it's going to come across. What if I don't say it right? What if it's misunderstood? What if I stir up an argument? Yet I never need worry about that with You. I can pour out my heart to You and it's safe—You will be a refuge for me.

Thank You, Lord Jesus, that no matter what I'm feeling, no matter how angry or frustrated or confused I am, and whether I make no sense at all, You listen. And You understand. And You are still there the next time I need to vent. Forgive me, Lord, for not coming to You first with all that is on my heart and mind. What heartache I would spare myself if You were always the first one I approached. I know You wait for me…and I don't want You to have to wait any longer.

The Lord Has Need of It

If anyone asks you, "Why are you untying it?"
you shall say, "The Lord has need of it."

LUKE 19:31

Lord, You are the Sovereign God of the Universe. You have need of nothing. Yet You asked Your disciples to untie a young donkey colt that had never been ridden so You could ride lowly and humbly into Jerusalem. You, the King, wanted something lowly from this earth, so that You could be exalted in a way that few understood. You, the King, asked for something humble so that You could be glorified.

Lord, what do You have need of in my life? My money? My possessions? My talents? My time? Those are things I might be proud to offer you. But something lowly? What lowliness do I have to offer the King? My insecurities? My pain? My discomfort? My weaknesses? Loosen my grip, Lord, so that I may untie whatever it is You have need of so that You can be glorified. I offer You my lowliness as a gift of love.

Your Burden Is Light

My yoke is easy and my burden is light.
MATTHEW 11:30

Jesus, when You saw Your people weighted down by all they felt they had to do to earn God's favor, You offered them *Your* burden instead—a burden You said was light. Yet the burden You placed on us—the one thing You required more than anything else—was for us to love You with all our heart, soul, and mind (Matthew 22:37). Lord, Your greatest requirement of us was not to *do* things for You. It was to *love* You above any person or thing. That is not a heavy burden. In fact, it's not a burden at all. It's a privilege.

Thank You, God, that the burden You place on me is not to work for my salvation or strive to earn Your love, but to love You with all that I am. For all the times I start to feel weary and weighted down, help me remember Your sweet, gentle invitation to come to You, lay my burden at Your feet, and find rest.

Renewed and Repaired

*Every part of Scripture is God-
breathed... Through the Word
we are put together and shaped up
for the tasks God has for us.*

2 TIMOTHY 3:16 MSG

Lord, that's what I need on those days when I don't
feel like facing all that I have to do. I need Your breath
of fresh air...that second wind from You. And I need
to be *put together and shaped up* for the tasks You have
for me. I need to be renewed and repaired—shaped up,
fixed up, wound up—so I can keep running properly
for You. And I know I can find that renewal and repair
in the pages of Your precious Word.

I can also find refreshment. As the psalmist says,
"Let your teachings breathe new life into me" (Psalm
119:25 CEV). Your Word says You are not only my "place
of quiet retreat" (Psalm 119:114 MSG), but also my "hiding place" (Psalm 32:7). So surely Your arms are where
I can go on those days when I need to be refreshed,
renewed, and rejuvenated. Now help me to get there—
every time.

You're Not Finished Yet

I am confident of this very thing, that
He who began a good work in you
will perfect it until the day of Christ Jesus.

Philippians 1:6 nasb

Lord, Your Word promises You will complete the work You have begun in me. That means You know all the unrefined parts of me that still need Your transforming touch. I am so grateful You are not giving up on me. You will not forget a thing. You have not declared me unworkable. You will not leave me unfinished.

It comforts me to know that You are aware of everything that is happening—and is yet to happen—in my life, to mold me and shape me into Your finished prize. I trust Your unseen heavenly hand and rest in the shadow of Your wings. In Your goodness, You allow nothing to touch my life that hasn't first gone through Your loving hands. I bank on that. I find encouragement in that. And I rest in that. I need no other answers as I've finally realized that You alone are the Answer.

Seeking You First

Seek first his kingdom and his righteousness,
and all these things will be given to you as well.

MATTHEW 6:33

Lord, You make it so simple. You tell me to seek You and Your kingdom first, and You will take care of all the things that I tend to worry about. Yet how I complicate life when I worry! I remember those days when I lost sleep worrying about finances, relationships I feared wouldn't last, and unforeseen circumstances. Yet as I have learned to seek You first, You have always taken care of everything else I've needed. *Everything.*

If You can care for my soul and secure it for eternity, certainly You can take care of the everyday details of my life. If You can reconcile my relationship with the Living God, certainly You can reconcile any earthly relationships as well. Help me to seek You first so I can honestly say, as the psalmist did: "The LORD is my shepherd, I lack nothing" (Psalm 23:1).

Seeking Your Face

My heart says of you, "Seek his face!"
Your face, LORD, I will seek.

PSALM 27:8

Lord, there are still days when I seek other things more than I seek You—more harmony in my marriage, a godly man for my daughter, a more fruitful ministry. Although the things I want are truly good…they are not enough. They have never, in and of themselves, satisfied. And they never will. Jesus, You must always be the *one thing* I want, or I will always long for something more. And while my heart cries out for You to change my circumstances or change the people in my life, I am the one You truly want to change.

Make me a woman who desires You more than anything else. You are the One who can "open your hand and satisfy the desires of every living thing" (Psalm 145:16). Strengthen me to wait upon You for the fulfillment of my desires. And when You become all I want, perhaps then I will be on my way to becoming all *You* want as well.

Hearing Your Voice

My heart has heard you say,
"Come and talk with me."
And my heart responds, "LORD, I am coming."

PSALM 27:8 NLT

Lord, there are times when my heart tells me I can wait no longer. I must be in Your presence. I must spend time with You. I must come back to the arms of the One who loves me more than any other. Yet that is You calling me, like the morning, to spend time in Your presence.

Forgive me, Lord, for the times I keep You waiting. Forgive me for not recognizing that the most important appointment of my day is meeting with the Living God of the Universe…and who am I to make You wait? Increase my longing to be with You so that I no longer keep You waiting. In fact, help me know what it means to wait for *You*. Help me to listen for Your whisper on my heart telling me to come and pray. As the psalmist sang, "My heart tells me to pray. I am eager to see your face" (Psalm 27:8 CEV).

You Are My Advocate

You are familiar with all my ways.
Before a word is on my tongue
you, LORD, know it completely.

PSALM 139:3-4

Lord, I love that You can see right through to my heart. You know my intentions. You know every time I mean well but don't express it, every time I mess up but didn't intend to, every time I'm misunderstood and miserable. You know. And You extend grace anyway.

As the psalmist sang,

> You have looked deep into my heart, LORD, and you know all about me. You know when I am resting or when I am working, and from heaven you discover my thoughts. You notice everything I do and everywhere I go. Before I even speak a word, you know what I will say, and with your powerful arm you protect me from every side. I can't understand all of this! Such wonderful knowledge is far above me (Psalm 139:1-6 CEV).

Surely You are my Great Advocate (1 John 2:1). May You sense my wonder of You throughout this day.

The God of All Comfort

He comforts us in all our troubles
so that we can comfort others.
When they are troubled, we will
be able to give them
the same comfort God has given us.

2 CORINTHIANS 1:4 NLT

Lord, You are not One who stands aloof with arms crossed waiting for me to learn a lesson and come crawling back to You. Scripture says You are the "Father of compassion and the God of all comfort, who comforts us in all our troubles, so that we can comfort those in any trouble with the comfort we ourselves receive from God" (2 Corinthians 1:3-4).

Thank You that You will never waste a wound. Or anything, for that matter. You recycle it and redeem it by giving me opportunities to pass on to others the same comfort You've given me in my times of disappointment and distress. Grant me Your eyes today to notice those who need a compassionate smile, a tender touch, a glimpse of Your grace so You can see Your gift of comfort passed on to someone else You want to touch today through me.

You Will Restore Me Once Again

Though you have made me see troubles,
many and bitter, you will restore my life again;
from the depths of the earth you
will again bring me up.
You will increase my honor and
comfort me once more.

PSALM 71:20-21

Lord, it's easy to look at the temporary—what I can see and hear and feel today—and forget about Your ongoing plan to restore my life in every way possible. Help me to remember that the difficulties I endure now are developing me into whom You want me to be later. My struggles today are making me stronger tomorrow. Today I will most likely encounter someone who is struggling in one way or another. Make me part of Your plan to give them comfort, encouragement, and hope for what You might possibly be wanting to do in their life. Thank You that I can comfort others with the comfort You've given me (2 Corinthians 1:4) and be a testimony to Your work in the lives of those You love.

Your Inseparable Love

Neither death nor life, neither angels nor demons,
neither the present nor the future, nor any powers,
neither height nor depth, nor
anything else in all creation
will be able to separate us from the love of God
that is in Christ Jesus our Lord.

ROMANS 8:38-39

Lord, at times my thoughts and fears try to separate me from Your love. That must be why You gave me a list, in Your Word, of what could never separate me from You. Your list makes me realize that even the things I struggle with cannot separate us—neither uncertainty nor unbelief, neither guilt nor shame, neither insecurity nor a sense of worthlessness. That makes me one loved lady!

You have searched my heart and You know me. And therefore You knew what I would need to hear—from Your Word—to be convinced of Your love for me. Just because others on this earth have let me down and broken my heart does not mean You ever will. I take refuge today in Your inseparable love.

As You Call Me Back

For your Maker is your husband—the Lord
Almighty is his name…
The Lord will call you back as if you were
a wife deserted and distressed in spirit.

ISAIAH 54:5-6

Jesus—Lover of my Soul—You know my whole history when it comes to relationships: the loves I've longed for, and those I've lost. And You tenderly tell me in Your Word that my Maker is my husband. How I needed to hear those words…and how I cherish them. Thank You that the God of this Universe, who knows all about me—my flaws and my failures, my worries and my weaknesses—still chooses to love me and call me His bride. No matter what I've been through, I know that my future is bright when You are the Love that is walking alongside me. It is time I acknowledge *You* as my spiritual husband. You are, after all, the only One on this earth who is truly able to say, "Never will I leave you" (Hebrews 13:5).

A Spacious Place

When hard pressed, I cried to the LORD;
he brought me into a spacious place.

PSALM 118:5

Lord, sometimes I long for a "spacious place" where I'm not so crowded in. A place where I can breathe deeply, hear Your voice, sense Your presence, and feel Your love.

I prefer my spacious place to be a relaxing vacation. But sometimes You usher me to a "spacious place" through a closed door, a layoff from work, or a cancelled appointment. Sometimes You allow an injury to slow me down or an illness to put me flat on my back, with nothing to do but listen for You. And sometimes You allow those times of aloneness as an open airy place to meet with You and hear Your voice again.

Lord, on the days that I complain about feeling alone, remind me of the spacious place You have blessed me with. I want to experience You as Your Word describes You: "solid rock under my feet, breathing room for my soul, an impregnable castle: I'm set for life" (Psalm 62:2 MSG).

All I Want

You, LORD, are all I want! You are my
choice, and you keep me safe.
You make my life pleasant, and
my future is bright.

PSALM 16:5-6 CEV

Lord, give me a heart like David the psalmist's so I will recognize that You are my greatest portion, possession, and inheritance. "The lines have fallen to me in pleasant places; indeed, my heritage is beautiful to me" (NASB).

Relationships, ambitions, or my desire for the next earthly "fix" can so easily consume my thoughts, dictate my actions, and become my purpose in life. But when *You* become all I want, I have found my treasure—and my song.

Please remove my unhealthy longings and replace them with a wholesome desire for You alone. May I be able to say, like David: "My choice is you, GOD, first and only. And now I find I'm your choice! You set me up with a house and yard. And then you made me your heir!" (Psalm 16:5-6 MSG).

The Object of Your Delight

His pleasure is not in the strength of the horse,
nor his delight in the legs of the warrior;
the LORD delights in those who fear him,
who put their hope in his unfailing love.

PSALM 147:10-11

Lord, You are not impressed with strong and mighty things, but with the meek and humble who admit they need You. Help me to have a wholesome dread of ever displeasing You. Help me to fear disappointing You more than I fear disappointing others. I want to live in that kind of reverence for You. If I am living complacently, not really needing You, nor fearing You, nor putting my hope in You, would You take me to a place in my circumstances where I *must* put my hope in You?

Thank You, Lord Jesus, for all You do in and around me to get me back to the place where I fear disappointing You. I long for You to delight in me as I put my hope in Your unfailing love.

My Shield and Glory

You, LORD, are a shield around me,
my glory, the One who lifts my head high.

PSALM 3:3

Lord, how often I underestimate or just don't appreciate Your shield around me. You shield me from the powers of darkness and the subtle allure of sin. You shield me from whatever might lead me astray. You shield me from the flaming arrows of the evil one (Ephesians 6:16). You shield me from far more than I will ever know. How many times have You closed a door I was not supposed to walk through because You knew far better than me what was on the other side? How many times have You shielded me from a person, place, or opportunity that I originally desired because You knew of the heartache that would follow? You are truly my shield and the One who lifts my head. You are the One who bestows glory and honor upon me, in Your way and in Your timing. You *are* my glory. You are my great reward.

An Undivided Heart

Teach me your way, LORD,
that I may rely on your faithfulness;
give me an undivided heart,
that I may fear your name.

PSALM 86:11

Lord, show me what I am relying on other than Your faithfulness. Show me what has become an idol in my life and keeps me from being wholly Yours. A dependence on money more than a dependence on You? A love of acceptance from others more than an assurance of Your acceptance of me? A desire for this world and its ways over a love for You and Your "eternal pleasures" (Psalm 16:11)?

I long for an undivided heart—one that relies on Your perfect track record of faithfulness. Then I will never look to anything or anyone else but You. Remove the idols from my heart, Lord. Seal it so it is wholly committed to You. As the psalmist prayed, "Train me, GOD, to walk straight; then I'll follow your true path. Put me together, one heart and mind; then, undivided, I'll worship in joyful fear" (Psalm 86:11 MSG).

Enlarge My Heart

I shall run the way of Your commandments,
for You will enlarge my heart.

PSALM 119:32 NASB

Lord, how I long to have an enlarged heart—to more deeply understand Your ways, to hold Your expansive wisdom, to live larger and more boldly for You. As I follow hard after You, set my heart free…

- from the love of self
- from the desire to be accepted
- from the trappings of busyness
- from the love of money
- from the petty distractions of this world
- from the need to succeed.

May my prayer echo the psalmist's heart:

> Barricade the road that goes Nowhere;
> grace me with your clear revelation.
> I choose the true road to Somewhere,
> I post your road signs at every curve and corner.
> I grasp and cling to whatever you tell me;
> GOD, don't let me down!
> I'll run the course you lay out for me
> if you'll just show me how (Psalm 119:29-32 MSG).

Nothing on My Own

*I do nothing on my own but speak just
what the Father has taught me.*

JOHN 8:28

Jesus, You set an example before me by doing nothing on Your own, but only what Your Father instructed. Oh, that that would characterize *my* life—*I do nothing on my own but speak just what the Father has taught me.* Yet there is often so much of me, so much of my agenda, so much of my own thoughts and words.

How much simpler and more focused my life would be if I were careful to do only what You instructed. I would have much more energy for the few things You wanted me to focus on. And I would be far less worn out from idle pursuits.

Oh, how I long to say, "I always do what pleases Him." Empower me with Your Holy Spirit, Lord Jesus, to speak and live in obedience to You so that many, as a result, will put their faith in You.

Your Love Chases Me

Surely your goodness and love will follow me
all the days of my life,
and I will dwell in the house of the LORD forever.

PSALM 23:6

In his twenty-third psalm, David recounted Your provision, Your protection, and Your unfailing love to him as a Good Shepherd. How You care for me too, God, by providing all I need (verse 1), making me rest when I need it (verse 2), guiding me along the right path (verse 3), providing comfort in the face of my fears (verse 4), and protecting me in the midst of my enemies (verse 5). And as if that weren't enough, You then send Your goodness and love to *follow* me for the rest of my life (verse 6). Lord, You are not obligated to do *anything* for me, yet You choose to bless me abundantly. Change my perspective today with the reminder that "Your beauty and love chase after me every day of my life." May my response be like that of David: "I'm back home in the house of GOD for the rest of my life" (verse 6 MSG).

Your Desires, My Delight

May he give you the desire of your heart
and make all your plans succeed.

PSALM 20:4

You, God, are the High and Mighty One. Your desires are all that matter. Your plans are the ones that must succeed. I could easily have destructive desires—temporary and tantalizing to my eyes, heart, and appetite. But Your desires, O God, are pure and right and lead to eternal life and joy.

Grant me *Your* desires, O Lord, so that the desire of my heart is the desire of *Your* heart as well. And present before me *Your* plans, O Lord, for I am weary of running after my own. Through me, may Your plans succeed. You say when I delight myself in You, You will give me the desires of my heart (Psalm 37:4). I delight in You, Lord—now place in my heart the desires You want me to have.

Calmed and Quieted

My heart is not proud, LORD,
my eyes are not haughty;
I do not concern myself with great matters
or things too wonderful for me.
But I have calmed and quieted myself,
I am like a weaned child with its mother;
like a weaned child I am content.

PSALM 131:1-2

Surely the Good Shepherd who leads me beside quiet waters (Psalm 23:2) and tells me to *be still* and know that He is God (Psalm 46:10) wants me to calm and quiet myself in His care. To rest in You, Lord, is to trust You to take care of all my questions and concerns. I long to be like a weaned child, content to just rest in Your arms, knowing full well You will provide for all I need and take care of all that concerns me. Be pleased, Lord, with my childlike trust in You. And as I calm myself and quiet my ambitions, whisper to me gentle reminders of Your power and Your love.

My Eyes Are on You

My eyes are ever on the LORD,
for only he will release my feet from the snare.

PSALM 25:15

As Your servant David prayed, "Show me your ways, LORD, teach me your paths. Guide me in your truth and teach me, for you are God my Savior, and my hope is in you all day long" (Psalm 25:4-5).

That is *my* prayer as well. I want to follow You closely…all day long. But there are snares all over my path today. Snares I can so easily fall into by simply walking in my own ability and not keeping my eyes on You. There is a trap of cynicism if I would engage in the negative talk. A pit of pride if I focus on my accomplishments. A rut of resentment if I entertain thoughts that should be forgotten. Only You, Lord, can release my feet from the snare and keep my mind focused on You and my heart fixed on love. Help me to remember, as the psalmist did: "If I keep my eyes on GOD, I won't trip over my own feet" (Psalm 25:15 MSG).

Your Great Wonders

To him who alone does great wonders,
his love endures forever.

<small>PSALM 136:4</small>

Lord, how it must thrill Your heart when, like a child, I live with a sense of wonder for You. Psalm 136 recounts how You made the heavens, spread out the earth upon the waters, and made the great lights—the sun to govern the day, and the moon and stars to govern the night. You brought Your people out of bondage by leading them through the midst of the sea and through the desert as well. You continue to give food to every living creature—the birds of the air and the fish of the sea. You are no different today, still aware of my need for deliverance, provision, and love.

Lord, don't let me get too serious, too practical, or so sophisticated in my ways that I don't see You as the big God that I once did. Remind me that my God is still great and mighty and there's nothing He cannot do. May I please Your heart by dreaming big, asking big, and expecting big things of You.

With Your Help

You, LORD, keep my lamp burning;
my God turns my darkness into light.
With your help I can advance against a troop;
with my God I can scale a wall.

PSALM 18:28-29

There are days I don't feel I can accomplish much. Help me to listen for Your whisper of assurance that "I can do all things through Christ who strengthens me" (Philippians 4:13 NKJV). You are the One who keeps my passion burning in the area of my convictions. You are the One who turns my darkness, despair, and even confusion into light. You are the One who helps me advance against a troop of insecurities, fears, or doubts. And with Your help I can scale a wall, no matter how high that wall of resistance may be.

I praise You, God, for being the One who keeps my lamp burning, my heart beating, and my hope churning. Grant me *Your* strength to advance against the troop that is coming at me and scale the wall that stands in my way.

Your Safety

In peace I will lie down and sleep,
for you alone, LORD,
make me dwell in safety.

PSALM 4:8

How often I succumb to the fears of this world, Lord, yet Your presence and protection is all around me. How often Your whispers of comfort keep me safe and secure. I can install a state-of-the-art alarm system in my home, but You alone, Lord, make me dwell in safety. I can hope my insurance plan will come through for me or put my trust in the amount of money in my bank account, but You alone, Lord, are my provision.

Your servant David was hunted all night long, yet he slept peacefully knowing You were His shield of protection. And You are the same God today who won't let my foot slip, who watches over me and neither slumbers nor sleeps (Psalm 121:3-4).

Loving Father, thank You for Your watchful eye, Your caring hand, Your saving arm, Your defending presence. May I please Your heart by trusting in You alone for my safety and provision.

Examine My Heart

All my longings lie open before you, Lord;
my sighing is not hidden from you.

Psalm 38:9

Lord, I love that You know all about me. And when You see desires of mine that are not fully in line with who You are and what You want for me, You do not toss me aside. You, instead, send friends my way to love me back to You. You send songs my way that remind me of where I need to be in my relationship with You. You send words my way that remind me that You are the One who opens Your hand and satisfies the desire of every living thing (Psalm 145:16). Lord, take any longing that lies within me that is unhealthy and replace it with a stronger desire for You. And because You tell me to "come boldly to the throne of grace" (Hebrews 4:16 NKJV) and tell You all that is on my heart, I will no longer try to hide anything from You.

Thank You, Lord, that You see it all and You love me just the same.

My Immovable Rock

Incline Your ear to me, rescue me quickly;
be to me a rock of strength,
a stronghold to save me.

PSALM 31:2 NASB

Lord God, You are my Rock of Strength and my Stronghold. I am so glad Scripture does not define You as my Driftwood, never in the same place twice. Or my Stream That Is Constantly Running. Or my Temperamental Power, in which I never know what to expect. Instead, Scripture says You are my Rock, my Refuge, my Strong Tower. Immovable. Unchanging. Steady. Always in the same place. I don't need to run after You and try to catch You. I don't need to try to find You because You've never left. And I don't need to constantly be on guard for fear that You might shift or change. You are my Rock, not my Roller Coaster—my *immovable Rock of Refuge to whom I can always go.*

On days when I feel like I'm on an emotional roller coaster with unpredictable moods, ups and downs in relationships, and ever-changing circumstances, remind me that I can find rest from my weariness in my Unchanging Rock.

The Wonders of Your Love

Praise be to the LORD,
for he showed me the wonders of his love
when I was in a city under siege.

PSALM 31:21

Lord, I have experienced days in which I felt like I was in a city under siege. Harsh words, accusations, and emotional outbursts all came flying my way. How I wanted to hide away in You and disappear. I was drained of energy. My heart was crushed. And yet You have shown me the wonders of Your love. You have assured me, in the midst of accusations, that I am Yours—bought with a price and fully justified by Your work on the cross—and therefore I need not rush to my own defense. You have shown me that whatever the situation, You are my Great Defender and Advocate. I praise You for loving me, protecting me, providing comfort when my heart feels ripped apart, and assuring me that I am Your child and therefore I am a new creation—the old is gone, the new has come. Where would I be were it not for the wonders of Your love?

Thirsting for You

As the deer pants for streams of water,
so my soul pants for you, my God.
My soul thirsts for God, for the living God.

PSALM 42:1-2

Lord, when I'm dry and weary of what this world has to offer, it is then that I understand the psalmist's desperation for You. I know what it's like to be "in the desert" and thirsty for more when it comes to relationships, finances, and even my desire to serve You, but feeling uncertain about my direction or purpose. But You, Lord, are the "more" I thirst for now. Nothing in and of this world will satisfy. Nothing will quench my longings and satisfy my soul like You and Your timely, healing Word.

As the deer longs for that mountain stream, I long for the living water of Your Word, the comfort of Your presence, the beauty of Your face. Thank You, Jesus, for Your invitation: "Let anyone who is thirsty come to me and drink" (John 7:37). Quench my thirst today with whispers from Your Word and assurances of Your presence.

The Light of Your Face

It was not by their sword that they won the land,
nor did their arm bring them victory;
it was your right hand, your arm,
and the light of your face, for you loved them.

PSALM 44:3

I have read of what You have done for Your people, O God, in giving them victory by Your right hand and by Your mighty arm. But giving Your people victory by "the light of your face"? And then I understood: "…for you loved them."

It is by "the light of Your presence" (NASB) that I have all that I have today. It is by Your "shining glory" (CEV) that I am able to succeed in what I do. It is by "the light of Your countenance" and because You "favored" me (NKJV) that I experience Your provision, Your protection, and Your innumerable blessings.

Lord, what do I have that hasn't been given to me from Your hands (1 Corinthians 4:7)? And to think that it is all because of the light of Your face, for You loved me.

My Stronghold

The LORD is my light and my salvation—
whom shall I fear?
The LORD is the stronghold of my life—
of whom shall I be afraid?

PSALM 27:1

I tend to think of a stronghold as something that has a debilitating grip on me. A destructive habit. A negative influence. A type of bondage. But You, God, are the Stronghold of my life—the One who has an empowering grip on me and keeps me safe, secure, and strong in You. I need not worry about losing my way when You go before me and light my path. I have no need to fear defeat when You are the One clearing the obstacles out of my way. Your Word says "If God is for us, who can be against us?" (Romans 8:31). And the answer is "neither death nor life…nor things present nor things to come… nor any other created thing, shall be able to separate us from the love [and protection] of God which is in Christ Jesus our Lord" (Romans 8:38-40 NKJV).

Thank You, Lord, for being the Stronghold of my life.

My Dwelling Place

Lord, you have been our dwelling place
throughout all generations.

Psalm 90:1

Lord, Your people wandered in the wilderness and You were their guiding presence in a cloud by day and in a pillar of fire by night. Then You settled in a tent in the wilderness and eventually a temple in Jerusalem, in the Most Holy of places where no one but a high priest could enter in. Yet today your Holy Spirit dwells in me—not in a temple or a tent, but in my heart.

Make Yourself at home in my heart, Lord Jesus. Kindle a warm fire in me that ever reminds me—and others—of the pure and perfect Guest who has come to dwell with me. And just as You make Yourself at home in my heart, help me to find my home in You. As Your servant David said, You are "the mighty rock that keeps me safe and the fortress where I am secure" (Psalm 62:2 cev).

On Things Above

*Set your minds on things above,
not on earthly things.*

Colossians 3:2

Lord, don't let me get too attached to the temporary things of this earth. You tell me not to store up treasures on this earth because they will be corrupted, destroyed, or stolen (Matthew 6:19-20). When I remember that everything I have here on earth is temporary—my possessions, my positions, my pain—and that my permanent address is Paradise, I am able to loosen my grip on the things of this world. I can part with possessions more easily. And I can blow off irritating matters that really don't matter in the scope of eternity.

Help me to walk confidently, with hope and expectation, by letting heaven fill my thoughts. May I be more careful how I treat others, more forgiving of how others have treated me, and more hopeful of the day I will finally be with Christ. Thank You that this earth is only my boot camp for heaven, my training for eternity. Help me to loosen my grip on the here and now and, instead, long for heaven and the hereafter.

My Living Hope

*He will wipe every tear from their eyes, and
there will be no more death or sorrow or crying
or pain. All these things are gone forever.*

REVELATION 21:4 NLT

Lord God, thank You that the "last chapter" of my life
is included in Your book. And it tells me I will someday
walk on streets of gold in a city more beautiful than my
mind can imagine. It tells me You will dwell with me
forever. And it tells me that my eternity will be without
any kind of pain, sorrow, or loss. What a legacy! And
what a hope to which I can cling! On those days when
loneliness begins to close in on me, remind me that it
is as temporary as the seasons of this life and the best is
yet to come. Lift my heart with the truth that my eternal life is already being lived and Your promise to never
let me walk alone is already in effect. I look forward to
the day You will walk me across that bridge from this
life into our long-awaited home together.

My Eternal Home

I am the Alpha and the Omega,
the First and the Last, the Beginning and the End.

<small>REVELATION 22:13</small>

Jesus, it all starts and ends with You. Your love was expressed for us in the Garden through a promise to come and die for us after man and woman sinned and left us a destiny of condemnation. You opened a new covenant era when You came to dwell among mankind and took the name "Emmanuel"—God with us. You gave up Your life, willingly, on a mount called Calvary to be our atoning sacrifice so You wouldn't have to live eternally without us. And today You reign on high, claiming us as Your bride and dwelling with us eternally.

Thank You that there exists no fear in death, no day without hope, no possibility of an existence without You. You are my beginning and my end as well. Upon finding me, You ensured that the old corruptible me ended and the new life I have in You began. Because of You alone I will never experience life apart from You. I will, instead, hear the whispers of Your love forever.

Surrendering Your Heart

If you have never accepted God's invitation of love through a personal relationship with Jesus, you can do that right now.

God's Word says we have all sinned (Romans 3:23), but through the death of His Son, Jesus, we can be forgiven of that sin and live in relationship with Him (Romans 6:23; Ephesians 2:8-9).

First, admit you are a sinner by nature and there is nothing you can do to make up for that sin in the eyes of a holy God. Second, accept the sacrifice that God provided—the death of His sinless Son, Jesus, on the cross on your behalf—in order to bring you into communion with Him.

Finally, enter into a love relationship with God, through your faith in Jesus, as a response to His love and forgiveness toward you. (For more on developing and maintaining an intimate relationship with God, see my book *Letting God Meet Your Emotional Needs* by Harvest House Publishers.)

If you have surrendered your heart to Christ, I would love to hear about it. Please email me at Cindi@StrengthForTheSoul.com. And welcome to His arms of love!

A Closing Word from Cindi

Thank you so much for reading *God's Whispers to a Woman's Heart*. I'm glad we've had this time together to get up close to His heart. Please visit my website at www.StrengthForTheSoul.com and leave me a note letting me know you were there. You can let me know how you've been encouraged by this book, find out more about my speaking ministry and other books, and sign up for my weekly blog or my free, monthly encouraging e-mails so we can keep in touch.

I hope to hear from you soon!
Cindi

Other Harvest House Books
by Cindi McMenamin

When a Mom Inspires Her Daughter

No matter what your daughter's age, God has given you a special and unique place from which to encourage, support, and inspire her. And there are many creative ways you can do that. Whether your girl is a child or an adult, or your relationship is strong or strained, this book offers a wealth of advice on ways you can enter your daughter's world and nurture a better relationship with her.

When Women Walk Alone

Every woman—whether she's single or married—has walked through the desert of loneliness. Whether you feel alone from being single, facing challenging life situations, or from being the spiritual head of your household, discover practical steps to finding support, transforming loneliness into spiritual growth, and turning your alone times into life-changing encounters with God.

Letting God Meet Your Emotional Needs

Do you long to have your emotional needs met, yet find that your husband or those close to you cannot always help bring fulfillment to your life? Discover true intimacy with God in this book that shows how to draw closer to the lover of your soul and find that He can, indeed, meet your deepest emotional needs.

When God Pursues a Woman's Heart

Within the heart of every woman is the desire to be cherished and loved. Recapture the romance of a relationship with God as you discover the many ways God loves you and pursues your heart as your hero, provider, comforter, friend, valiant knight, loving daddy, perfect prince, and more.

When Women Long for Rest

Women today are tired of feeling overwhelmed by all the demands on their lives and are longing for rest. They want to do more than just simplify or reorganize their lives. *When Women Long for Rest* is an invitation for women to find their quiet place at God's feet—a place where they can listen to Him, open their hearts to Him, and experience true rest.

When a Woman Discovers Her Dream

When it comes to living out the dream God has placed on your heart, do you shrug your shoulders and say, "It's too late…it's too far out of reach…it's too impossible for someone like me"? But you *can* live out that dream—no matter what your stage or place in life. Join Cindi as she shares how you can explore God's purposes for your life, make greater use of your special gifts, turn your dreams into reality, and become the masterpiece God designed you to be.

When a Woman Inspires Her Husband

How can you become your husband's number one fan? God brought you alongside him in marriage to love and support him as only a wife can. Discover how you can be the encourager, motivator, inspiration, and admiration behind your husband—and the wind beneath his wings—as you understand his world, become his cheerleader, appreciate his differences, ease his burdens, and encourage him to dream.

When a Woman Overcomes Life's Hurts

Only God can take the bitter things and turn them into blessings. But healing cannot take place until you uproot the faulty thinking that often accompanies life's wounds and replace it with the truth about how God views you. You'll find this book filled with grace, redemption, and transformation that leads you toward a renewed focus on God, a resurgence of inner joy, and better relationships with others.

When You're Running on Empty

Are you feeling run down and ready to give up? If so, then you're probably running on empty. And you may feel as if the pressures and stress will never end. But there is a way out. Cindi shares from her own life and struggles many helpful and practical secrets about simplifying your priorities and obligations, rejuvenating yourself through God's Word, cultivating health habits that renew your energy, and learning to please God and not people.

Women on the Edge

We all have times when we find ourselves on the verge of frustration, despair, or even a meltdown. And we find ourselves at a crossroads: One path cries out for us to escape it all. The other calls us to persevere and lean on the Lord. Rather than merely survive, choose to abundantly thrive—by learning how to yield all control of your life to God, rest in His purpose and plan for your life, and enjoy the confidence of a heart wholly surrendered to Him.

When Couples Walk Together
(with Hugh McMenamin)

Are the demands of everyday life constantly pulling you and your spouse in different directions? If you've longed to rekindle the intimacy and companionship that first brought you together, join Hugh and Cindi McMenamin as they share 31 days of simple, creative, and fun ways you can draw closer together again. You'll find your marriage greatly enriched as you experience anew the joys of togetherness and unselfish love.

To learn more about Harvest House books and
to read sample chapters, log on to our website:

www.harvesthousepublishers.com

HARVEST HOUSE PUBLISHERS
EUGENE, OREGON